To Barbara Leapman Goldberg

*May her memory always be a blessing
and her life a beautiful lesson.*

contents

introduction

There's no such thing as "too much yarn."

In fact, if you just mention the word *stash* to any knitter or crocheter, you'll likely get a slightly mischievous grin in response. "Oh, you mean my 'yarn reserves,'" one might quip. "I could never accumulate enough!" Some even joke that whoever dies with the biggest hoard wins. . . .

So we collect it. Lots of it. And we love it. Unabashedly. In fact, our stash (not to mention its size) is often a favorite topic of conversation.

Some of this treasured collection consists of one or two extra balls of yarn purchased "just in case." Much of it is just partial balls—precious bits and pieces left over from completed projects. Then there are those times a single ball of this or that lands in the stash because it's something you are curious to try out, or perhaps it was an irresistible bargain, happily discovered in a hidden sale bin. And who can resist picking up yarn as a souvenir from vacations and business trips? (As much as we all love our local yarn shops, it's fun to spread our yarn budget around. I bet I'm not the only one who looks up LYS's in the phone book first thing upon arriving at an out-of-town hotel!)

But our beloved stash somehow stirs a sense of guilt. It's a love/hate relationship. As much as we secretly enjoy that occasional midnight "Dive Into the Reservoir of Treasure" (DIRT), we also struggle to "Whittle All Stash on Hand" (WASH). We gaze upon the piles and bags and bins and sometimes think it's a waste, that there's just so much potential in there, if only we could figure out what to do with it.

Some of the challenge comes from a lack of organization. How many times have you come across a yarn in your stash and thought I don't even remember buying that or I forgot I had that? Knowing what is already sitting in your stash will prevent needless duplication, and similar yarn types kept together make mixing and matching easy and satisfying. Most important, a knitter must be able to locate just

"Oh, you mean my 'yarn reserves,'" one might quip. "I could never accumulate enough!" Some even joke that whoever dies with the biggest hoard wins.

the perfect ball at a moment's notice (often just seconds before the ideal needle-clicking movie starts on TV). A well-organized stash will empower you. Trust me!

Part One of this book addresses practical yet fun ways to store and arrange the stash so it is tidy, protected (from moths, that is, not robbers), convenient, easy to use, and most important, inspirational. You'll find a complete discussion on how to choose and work with different yarns, with a special emphasis on how to create surefire color combinations. No one ever said that scrap happy had to mean haphazard!

But the question remains how to make the best use of your trove of beautiful yarns. Never fear! Part Two contains twenty-one projects and loads of ideas, all designed to use up that stash. There are projects both large and small, from a make-it-in-one-evening hat (Rick Rack, on page 111) to a dramatic, fashion-runway-worthy jacket

Let's begin putting that stash to good use! Remember, as each bit of stash is used up, there will be room to buy even more!

that'll provide weeks of knitting enjoyment (Roundabout, on page 93). There's a chapter for each yarn weight, from super fine to super bulky, ensuring that no yarn will be left to languish—not even that partial ball of itchy, mop-colored mohair. (Amazingly, even that can be transformed when mixed nicely with other treasures into a "magic ball.") Now how's that for knitting green and being thrifty at the same time?

To help you customize projects, DIY (Design It Yourself) sections are offered throughout the book, and Scrap Happy notes in every pattern will make it easy for you to use every precious morsel of stored-up yarn, whether you own a few yards or a whole bag.

Best of all, each project is cleverly designed so that no one will ever suspect it was made from leftovers!

If you're new to knitting (or just want some refresher material), turn to techniques (page 128). It contains all the knitting information necessary to ensure success as you turn yarn bought last week or long ago into exciting new projects.

So dive into your closets, dig into your bins, rifle through your drawers, and crawl under your bed. Let's begin putting that stash to good use! Remember, as each bit of stash is used up, there will be room to buy even more!

part one

it's not just a stash,

it's a personalized yarn collection!

I like to think of a person's yarn stash as his or her own personal yarn shop, a truly customized supply of fiber and materials. After all, each component is already well loved: it's either yarn left over from a finished project or else is a glorious treasure discovered (and then hoarded) for future use.

At its best, this cornucopia of color and texture offers the convenience of discovering just the right yarn exactly when you need it rather than on the day after a knitting project has already been completed (been there, done that!); at its worst, it's a dust-collecting, messy eyesore.

To put your stash to good use, it's important to take the time to organize and store its precious contents so it is manageable, easy to use, and most important, *inspirational.*

If you arrange your stash the way most local yarn stores organize their inventory, it will excite you and stimulate your creativity endlessly. Just follow these steps!

Let's face it: You can't organize your stash without being intimately familiar with everything you own. You must drag all of it out into the open so you can see it. So be strong, and locate every single skein of it—even those little bits and pieces you've tucked away.

The size of your stash will determine how long this step will take. It could take an afternoon, a weekend, or even longer. It all depends on how much you've got, and only you know that.

Make it an adventure, and haul every last bit of yarn into one well-lit place—a spare bedroom, the corner of your living room, or the middle of your craft room, if you're lucky enough to have one.

If you have kids or pets, be sure to keep them away from your exposed stash, especially during this preliminary stage, when everything is just heaped on the floor. (Need I tell you that a $2,500 vet bill for kitty abdominal surgery a few years ago was the impetus for organizing and securing my yarn once and for all!)

Sort It

Once it is assembled (and has totally messed up your work area), it's time to organize your stash by weight and color. (I recommend that you not even think of starting this yarn organizational process if you're supposed to be working or doing some other important thing. Unless it's a knitting book about stash.)

To begin, separate the yarn according to yarn **weight**. Most local yarn shops display their yarn this way because that's how commercial knitting patterns list items in materials lists. It makes sense that if a customer's pattern designates worsted-weight yarn for a project, that knitter will find it easier to find the perfect yarn by browsing only the shelves that hold worsted-weight yarn rather than looking through the entire store. You'll be shopping your stash in a similar way.

Make four separate piles: super fine and fine (CYCA categories 1 and 2); light (CYCA category 3); medium (CYCA category 4); bulky and super bulky (CYCA categories 5 and 6).

To determine the yarn weight, check the yarn label to see the manufacturer's suggested gauge, then refer

CYCA category	1	2	3	4	5	6
Yarn Weight	Lace, Fingering, Sock	Sport	DK, Light Worsted	Worsted, Aran	Chunky	Bulky, Roving
Avg. Knitted Gauge over 4"/[10cm]	27–32 sts	23–26 sts	21–24 sts	16–20 sts	12–15 sts	6–11 sts
Recommended Needle (U.S. Sizes)	1–3	3–5	5–7	7–9	9–11	11 and larger
Recommended Needles (Metric Sizes)	2.25–3.25mm	3.25–3.75mm	3.75–4.5mm	4.5–5.5mm	5.5–8mm	8 mm and larger

to the chart for the Craft Yarn Council of America's Standard Yarn Weight System.

If a ball of yarn has no label, use the wraps-per-inch (WPI) system to categorize its weight. A handy WPI tool is marketed to weavers and handspinners, but if you don't have one, it's easy to make your own. Just find an unsharpened pencil or narrow dowel (or even an old-fashioned wooden ruler), and make two slash marks exactly 1"/[2.5cm] apart. Wrap your mystery yarn around your tool, carefully arranging the strands so they are right next to each other with no overlap. Count the number of strands between your two marks to determine the WPI. See the chart at right to find the corresponding yarn weight.

For greater accuracy, especially for thick yarns, make your slash marks 2"/[5cm] apart. Count the number of strands between the two marks and divide by 2 to determine the WPI.

Number of wraps per inch (WPI)	Yarn weight
19 or more	Super fine
15–18	Fine
12–14	Light
9–11	Medium
7–8	Bulky
6 or fewer	Super bulky

 *scrap happy*

Just because a yarn possesses a particular weight doesn't mean you're limited to using it as is!

■ *Yarns that are plied can be carefully untwisted and separated into individual strands of lighter-weight yarns. (This tip is best used for small amounts of yarn, since those newly released strands tend to become quite tangled and unwieldy. Don't ask me how I know.)*

■ *Finer-weight yarns can be combined to create thicker ones (see the Bravissimo Throw on page 125, for example). Simply hold two or even three strands of yarn together and use them as one. Refer to the chart for substitution information. Note that these are approximations, since every knitter's tension is different and each yarn has its own twist and hardness. For the best results, knit a swatch holding your multiple strands together and measure your resulting gauge.*

To get this yarn weight:	Combine these strands of yarn:
1 strand of light	2 strands of super fine
1 strand of medium	1 strand of super fine + 1 strand of fine
1 strand of medium	1 strand of super fine + 1 strand of light
1 strand of medium	3 strands of super fine
1 strand of medium	2 strands of fine
1 strand of bulky	3 strands of fine
1 strand of bulky	1 strand of fine + 1 strand of light
1 strand of bulky	1 strand of super fine + 1 strand of medium
1 strand of bulky	1 strand of fine + 1 strand of medium
1 strand of bulky	2 strands of light
1 strand of bulky	1 strand of light + 1 strand of medium
1 strand of super bulky	1 strand of super fine + 1 strand of bulky
1 strand of super bulky	1 strand of fine + 1 strand of bulky
1 strand of super bulky	1 strand of light + 1 strand of bulky
1 strand of super bulky	2 strands of medium
1 strand of super bulky	2 strands of bulky

Note: You'll be a happier knitter if you work from several individual balls of yarn rather than rewinding your yarn into a single multistranded ball. Otherwise, one of the yarns might "feed" at a different rate and cause frustration later. Trust me.

Once you've separated your yarns by weight, further divide the piles according to **color**. Ideally, you will create subsections for each yarn weight, one for each hue on the color wheel on page 17: yellow, yellow-orange, orange, red-orange, red, red-violet, violet, blue-violet, blue, blue-green, green, and yellow-green. Toss all the yellows, for instance, into one heap; all the yellow-oranges into another, etc. Put variegated, hand-dyed, and novelty yarns in the piles with the closest color match. Create separate groupings for black, white, and gray.

If your stash is small (I mean, "young") and your storage space is limited, combine all the cool colors together in one heap and the warm colors in another, with separate piles for black and white. You'll find it more inspiring to see a few balls of red and orange lumped together rather than a single ball of this or that. Refer to the color wheel to determine the temperature of specific colors.

Refer to pages 18–20 to learn ways to work with and to combine colors in your stashbusting projects. There's no reason your precious knitting—even when made from leftover yarn—needs to appear hodgepodge and scrappy!

Catalog It

Like all the goodies in your favorite yarn shop, your stash will be most effective if you take a physical inventory of it. Here are some suggestions:

- Check out www.ravelry.com. It's a comprehensive resource for all things knitting and crochet. One of its most useful features helps you catalog your stash (and needle) inventory. Even technological neophytes will find the process easy—just click on the "stash" button under the My Notebook tab and follow the directions. There's even a space to indicate where you've stored the yarn! (As I mentioned, this information will definitely come in handy.) Sure, it might take a while to input everything if you have a prodigious stash, but it will be worth it.

- Use a database to computerize your stock: Several software programs are available to help you keep track of the ebb and flow of your stash. Be sure to update it—the contents, I mean, not just the software—to reflect your current holdings.

- Download an app for your smartphone or iPad so you can have a complete listing with you every time you shop. Check to see if you really need those three balls of acid-green cotton that are on sale—or if you already have some languishing in your stash.

- Create a special yarn notebook, a personal journal that lists every yarn you own. Take it from She-Who-Owns-the-World's-Largest-Yarn-Stash-While-Living-in-a-New-York-City-Apartment: Sometimes you'll want to see and touch your precious goodies without having to actually haul everything out of its carefully arranged space. (Especially if it's literally crammed floor-to-ceiling with little room to maneuver the bins!) It's great to refer to your notebook when planning new projects—and use it for inspiration when you're between them. Use a three-ring binder with clear page protectors with pockets for trading cards. Insert a snippet of yarn along with notes into each little compartment. It wouldn't hurt to include a clear description of the yarn's most recent storage location as well (don't ask). It's easy to add pages as your stash grows. Or purchase a pretty, bound scrapbook and make an entry for each yarn, taping snippets onto the pages to relate color and texture.

Store It

Quick, before your sweet, adorable kitten begins carrying—and then hiding!—your yarn treasure everywhere, you'll have to make some decisions regarding storage. Now that you can actually see the amount of yarn you own, it's time to determine where and how you will store it.

If you can devote an entire room to your stash, lucky you! If not, some space in a closet or under the bed will work nicely. Will you keep it out in the open (after all, nothing impresses a knitter more than the size—and tidiness—of another's stash) or will you tuck everything away?

For storage, use one or more of the following options (since just tossing the yarn willy-nilly into a closet is not recommended).

First, resist using lawn and leaf garbage bags for storage. Sure, they're already conveniently sitting on your pantry shelf, just waiting to be used, but the thin plastic won't hold up to habitual stash-diving. Just take my word for it. Instead, pack your yarn in something more durable.

Zip-top storage bags come in lots of sizes (from small enough to tame a single ball of unruly eyelash yarn to others large enough for some folks' entire stash). They're strong, inexpensive, will protect your yarn from dust and critters, and are flexible enough to fit in places boxes and bins can't. The superlarge ones even have built-in handles!

Another idea is to recycle those heavy-duty plastic zippered bags that linens and comforters come in. If you fill them completely, their gusseted sides allow them to stack on top of one another beautifully.

Of course, space-saving vacuum bags are a good solution for small spaces. As a bonus, with all the air sucked out inside them, they have less of a chance of harboring moths and other critters.

You can neatly store all your bags (or even your bare yarn) in plastic tubs with snap-on tops. Most are stackable, so it's easy to arrange them vertically to make the best use of space. You can build custom shelves to accommodate them in a closet or else keep your bins out in the open. Having your stash visible will likely inspire you to use it—after all, who could resist all that color and texture?

Drawers are suitable only if they come completely out; it's handy to be able to carry your materials close to your actual workspace. (Especially during those midnight forays into your stash.) Besides, the one ball of yarn you are most desperately looking for will likely be the one in the back of a drawer, all the way on the bottom, right?

Keep in mind that opaque is better than crystal clear, especially if the containers will be stored in a bright spot. Sunlight can do a real number on many dyes. (In my south-facing apartment, for example, my beautiful burgundy sofa has been sun-bleached to a milky terracotta.) The bins I prefer are frosted, allowing me to see the contents while still protecting the yarn from strong light. If you must use cardboard boxes, be sure to label the specific contents on the outside.

If space is limited, under-the-bed containers can be useful. In this case, either cardboard or plastic will do, but if you go this route, be sure to choose ones with secure lids. Yarn already gets enough cat hair added to it during the knitting stage.

Some creative knitters store their yarn in hanging shoe organizers inside a closet or over a door. Others utilize wine bottle racks. (Why store wine when you can store yarn?) Of course, tiered hanging fruit baskets offer a pretty way to store—and display—yarn.

Furniture stores, office supply companies, or even your local flea market will offer you other storage ideas. Be creative!

Protection from Moths and Other Nasties

If not stored properly, your stash could be vulnerable to moths, mold, and other critters. Use these suggestions to safeguard your precious stash:

- If you live in a particularly humid area, store your yarns, especially those made of natural fibers, in a cool, dehumidified room to prevent mold. At the first sign of a problem, follow the laundering instructions on the label, and wash the yarn, allowing it to dry completely before putting it back into dry storage.

- Clothing moths are attracted to the fiber in our yarns, so it's important to take some precautions. Ditch those old-fashioned stinky mothballs and tuck some environmentally friendly aromatic herbs into your storage areas instead. Lavender, clove, and cedar are effective. And since herbal essential oils lose their potency in time, remember to refresh your supply at least once a year; cedar blocks will lose their scent over time, but will be just like new if you give them a very light sanding. You can even use a small bit of your stash to knit a tiny pillow or pouch to use as a sachet! (Remember, using up stash creates room for more.)

If you've already discovered a moth infestation, don't panic. Freeze the affected yarn at 10°F or below for several days to kill the pests. Bring it back to room temperature to allow potential eggs to hatch, and then refreeze it to kill the larvae.

Help! My Stash Runneth Over!

If you own more stash than you can possible store (let alone *use in one lifetime*), you must reel things in. Try the following suggestions to cull your collection.

■ Throw a "stash bash" for you and your friends. Invite everyone to your place (since you have so much yarn to spare), and swap yarn. After all, one person's trash is another's treasure! One cardinal rule: No one goes home with anything they brought along; all remaining yarn will be donated to charity (see below). And don't leave your faraway cyberfriends out! Destash on the internet using ravelry.com, eBay.com, or various yarn-swapping lists on yahoo.com.

■ Make a gift of your excess stash to those who will truly appreciate it. Many schools, prisons, social services organizations, senior centers, and other community associations will gladly accept yarn. And to increase the value of your donation, volunteer a few hours of your time to teach those lucky folks to knit or crochet.

■ Use your leftovers to make warm and cozy items for charity. Many organizations do important work nationally, including the Warm Up America Foundation (www.warmupamerica.org), Hugs for Homeless Animals (www.h4ha.org/snuggles), the Project Linus Organization (www.projectlinus.org), and the Ships Project for Troop Support (www.theshipsproject.com). Better yet, research local charities so you can spread your love closer to home.

■ Use yarns that are especially pretty as decorative ribbon or for bows when wrapping gifts. One ball of novelty yarn will enliven a lot of packages!

■ If you make stuffed animals and toys, use bits and pieces of leftover yarn to stuff them. Tuck in some potpourri (or catnip in certain cases, lavender in others) for a special touch.

■ Learn a new fiber-related craft such as crochet, handweaving, or appliqué. Discovering a different use for your old materials might just stimulate your creativity; that awful gray, worming bulky-weight chenille might make terrific doll hair!

■ Make colorful tassels to decorate your home. Use yarn left over from afghans and throws to create accents that coordinate perfectly with each room!

■ Why not make gobs of pom-poms and sew them onto purchased scarves, hats, pillows, and other items for personalized pizzazz? A handy tool is commercially available that ensures they're always fat and neatly trimmed.

■ Braid several strands of stash yarn together to make cool bracelets, belts, and nonstretchy straps for handbags.

If you choose your colors wisely, it'll be your secret that a project was created from leftovers. Here's how.

Scientific Theory

I'll bet Sir Isaac Newton never thought he'd be mentioned in a knitting book, but his formulation of the color wheel in the late seventeenth century can help all of us—even the timid—create beautiful and interesting color schemes. Want a refresher course on basic color theory? Here is everything a knitter needs to know.

The color wheel shows the relationship between the twelve colors of the spectrum: yellow, yellow-orange, orange, red-orange, red, red-violet, violet, blue-violet, blue, blue-green, green, and yellow-green. It's easy to use each color's location on the circle to design harmonious palettes. In fact, if you ever encounter some hideous shade of orange in the sale bin of your local yarn shop and you still must have it (we've all been there), use it within one of these official, scientifically ordained color combinations, and it will shine!

Monochromatic Color Combinations

Monochromatic colorways consist solely of variations of a single hue. But don't for a minute think that because just one color is used the effect must be boring! Sea of Blue on page 71 is a rich array of blues. And even shades of white and cream can appear dramatic (see the Alternative Colorway 1 for Roundabout on page 93).

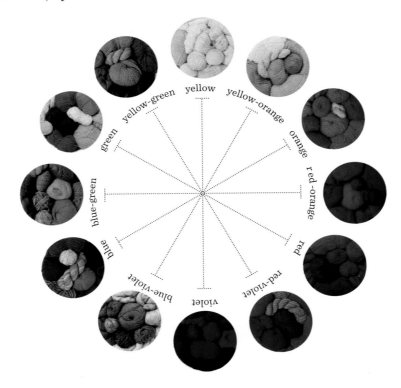

Two-Color Combinations

Complementary Colors

Colors directly across from each other on the color wheel are known as complementary colors. This kind of combination, such as yellow and violet, creates lots of contrast within a project. (a)

Counterpoint Colors

In this type of combination, like blue-violet with yellow-orange, for example, a color is teamed up with one of the colors on either side of its direct complement across the color wheel. Here, the effect is fresh and modern. (b)

Three-Color Combinations

Triad Colors

This color scheme uses three hues that are equidistant from one another on the color wheel. The three primary colors (red, blue, and yellow) comprise one triad, and the three secondary colors (orange, green, and violet) make up another. Because of the range of temperatures involved (cool blues and greens to warm yellows and reds), designs using this sort of palette seem especially balanced. (c)

Split Complementary Colors

One color combined with each of the two colors on either side of its direct complement makes up this kind of combination. Yellow, green, and red-violet comprise one example. (d)

Analogous Colors

Three colors that are next to each other on the color wheel are called analogous colors. Tamara's Wrap on page 97, for instance, uses this sort of colorway. Notice how rich the fabric appears. (e)

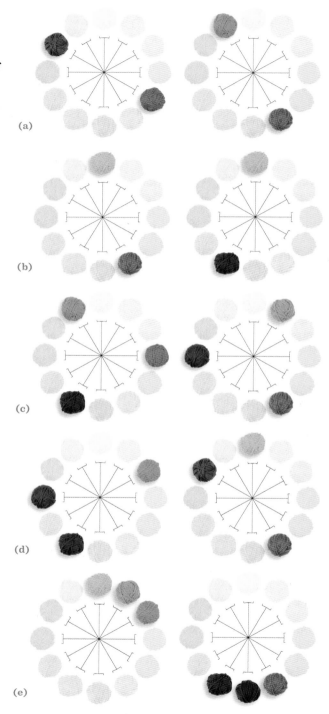

(a)

(b)

(c)

(d)

(e)

Four-Color Combinations

Square Tetrad Colors

Two sets of equidistant complementary colors create a square tetrad combination. Sausalito on page 83, with its yellow-green, orange, red-violet, and blue hues uses one possible square tetrad colorway. **(f)**

Rectangular Tetrad Colors

Two pairs of complementary colors that create a rectangular shape on the color wheel are called rectangular tetrads. Try implementing this type of colorway in your own stripe pattern when knitting Sporty Stripes on page 61. **(g)**

Analogous Colors with a Complement

Combine three adjacent colors on the color wheel plus the complementary color directly across from them to create this type of palette. The Alternative Colorway 1 for the Fire and Ice Cozy Cowl on page 39 uses several variations of red, red-orange, red-violet, and green and exemplifies this sort of color scheme. **(h)**

Double Complementary Colors

Two adjacent colors on the color wheel, along with both of their complements, are called double complementary colors. One example is the combination of violet, yellow, blue-violet, and yellow-orange. **(i)**

Five-Color Combinations

Double Split Complementary Colors

One color plus the two hues on each side of that color's complement make up this combination. Red-orange, green, yellow-green, blue, and blue-violet represent one set of double split complementary colors. Try implementing this kind of color scheme in the Toasty design on page 57. **(j)**

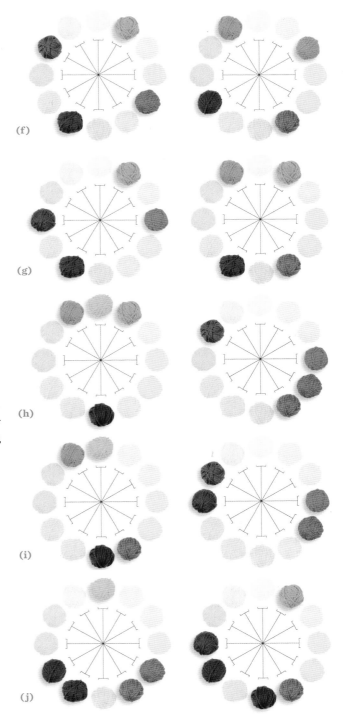

(f)

(g)

(h)

(i)

(j)

Six-Color Combinations

Double Triad Colors

This type of colorway consists of two sets of triads, one adjacent to the other. Like the triad combinations, the varying color temperatures ensure balance and harmony, as in a grouping of yellow-green, green, blue-violet, violet, orange, and red-orange. **(k)**

Hexad Colors

This grouping combines three pairs of complementary colors that are all equidistant from one another; in other words, a hexad uses every other color on the color wheel. One possible hexad combination is blue, green, yellow, orange, red, and violet. **(l)**

Of course, using scientific color theory to choose a palette is an easy way to create successful and pleasing combinations, but it surely isn't the only—or even the best—way.

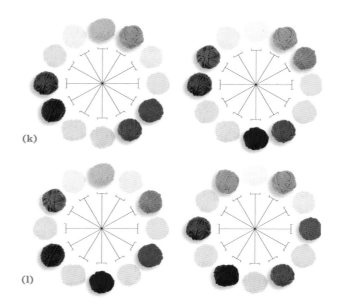

A More Subjective Approach

Obviously, we don't need science to validate our personal color sense; sometimes particular color palettes simply feel *right*. We can use our innate creativity and natural curiosity to create perfectly lovely combinations. Here are some jumping-off points:

- For a foolproof color scheme, choose one that's found in nature. You won't be the first: Artists and designers have copied the Master Creator for ages. Alternative Colorway 2 for Sausalito on page 83, for example, uses colors plucked from an evening sunset.

- Grab a mix of autumnal hues. Alternative Colorway 2 for the Fire and Ice Cozy Cowl on page 39 uses this type of color combination. Knit an item with these colors and you just know it will keep out the chill!

- Blend together neutrals, such as those seen in Amy's Sleeveless Hoodie on page 119, and you'll create a garment that will coordinate with nearly everything you own. The Alternative Colorway 1 for the Greenmarket Bag on page 35 is another go-with-all color combination. And Alternative Colorway 2 for Sea of Blue on page 71 combines twenty-seven natural shades that any man in your life will love—and actually wear.

- A grouping of tropical brights is always energetic and fun. See Alternative Colorway 2 for Roundabout on page 93.

- Choose tints of several colors—called pastels—to create a soft and serene palette. Add white if you'd like some contrast and eye movement.

When you're using bits and pieces of lots of different colors within a single project, you'll often want to create a sense of unpredictability and randomness. It adds eye movement and visual excitement. Refer to the following ideas to keep your patterns interesting.

Magic Ball Technique

Combine several short lengths of different colors (and often textures!) of yarn into one long piece of yarn that's surprisingly fun to knit with. It's like having a completely customized ball of variegated yarn! Knitters have two ways of joining the yarns: either quickly with overhand knots or more smoothly using the Russian join.

To Create a Magic Ball Using Knots

Cut a random length (usually between 12 and 36"/[30.5 and 91.5cm]) of the first yarn and wind it into a ball. Cut a slightly different length of a second yarn, and use an overhand knot to tie it to the first piece (illustration 1). You can make the yarn tails coming out of the knots whatever length you like, however I usually trim them to ³⁄₄"/[1.5cm] or so.

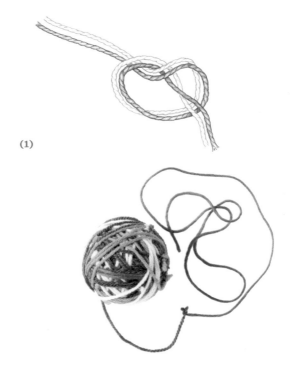

(1)

Wind this new piece of yarn around the same ball as the first one.

Continue adding random lengths of different yarns to create a single length of knittable yarn.

Amazingly, when the magic ball is knitted in stockinette stitch, the knots will automatically end up on the wrong side, the purl side, of the fabric. Or you can even use the trimmed knots as a planned design feature in reverse stockinette fabrics!

To Create a Magic Ball Using the Russian Join

If both sides of your fabric are going to show in your project and you'd rather not have the knots exposed (as in Mona's Little Bias Scarf on page 41 and in the collar section of Roundabout on page 93), use this technique to make a smooth magic ball without knots.

Make a loop in one of the yarn ends by threading its tail onto a sharp-tipped needle and drawing it back through an inch or two of itself, making certain it's woven within the plies of the yarn, looping one end of the next length of yarn as you begin (illustration 2).

Remove the needle, leaving the loop (illustration 3).

Keeping it interlocked to the first yarn, thread the second yarn end onto the needle and run this yarn back through its own plies, as you did the first one (illustration 4), then tug on the ends to tighten them, and then trim them.

Continue to add new yarns in this fashion, being careful to vary the lengths as you go.

These magic balls are fun ways to combine bits and pieces of your stash into an artist's material. Every stitch of knitting will offer another exciting surprise!

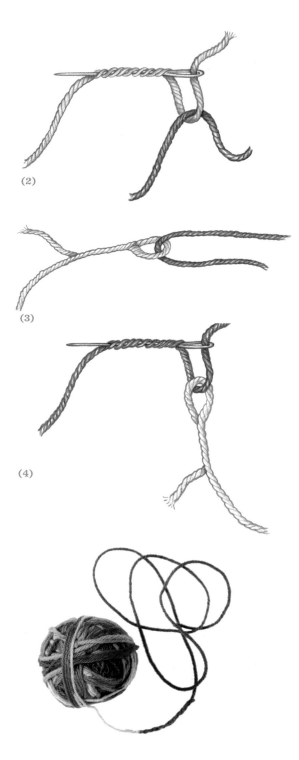

(2)

(3)

(4)

More Math and Science

Mathematical formulas, such as the Golden Mean and the Fibonacci sequence, can cut out the guesswork for proportions and add a mysteriously pleasing aesthetic to knitting designs.

The Golden Mean

The special irrational number, 1.618034, has been used for centuries by musicians, artists, and others to develop dimensional proportions. If it was good enough to help the Greeks to build the Parthenon, it will surely add balance and structure to your knitting. Try using it to create interesting striping patterns or to calculate the perfect dimensions for any rectangular blocks of solid color within a project. When making a patchwork afghan, for example, make your motifs 13 x 8" rather than 12 x 8" to take advantage of the magic!

The Fibonacci Sequence

In this mathematical series, each successive number is the sum of its two predecessors: 0, 1, 1, 2, 3, 5, 8, 13, 21, etc. To use it when planning color sequences, choose several numbers from the series and use them to develop a stripe pattern.

Use One Color as a Base

To create a harmonious color scheme out of seemingly dissimilar hues, knit your project using two strands of yarn held together, carrying one color throughout the entire piece while randomly changing the contrast color as you go. The double-stranded project will knit up faster, making room in your stash for new goodies. Bonus!

Or alternate several contrast colors with a single main color throughout the project, as seen in the Greenmarket Bag on page 35. In this case, the recurring green stripes make all six colors appear anchored and balanced. Often, designers use black, white, navy, or gray this way.

Take a Chance!

For fun, devise a dice game to create a pattern. Make a list of twelve colors of yarn you'd like to use in a project, and number each one. Roll the dice once to determine what color to use, then roll them again to see how many rows (or stitches) to work for that particular color. (As if knitting weren't exciting enough!)

Here's another idea: Toss appropriate yarns into a large bag. When it's time in your stripe pattern to change colors, simply insert your hand and grab a ball of yarn! (No cheating, either—make a pact with yourself that you'll use whatever color emerges. Random means random.)

Of course color isn't the only consideration when shopping your stash. Laundering instructions, weight, and the actual amount required are all important.

The Least Common Denominator

Be sure that each yarn used within a project has the same laundering and care specifications. Nothing could be worse than having one of your stripes shrink while another stretches. (Unless you were intentionally striving for a ruched effect!) Read all yarn labels carefully, and if in doubt, choose the most conservative laundering method. Hand-washing in cold water and laying flat to dry seems to work in most cases.

Size Matters

Every project calls for a certain weight of yarn, one that will yield the exact gauge specified in its pattern. The designs in this book are arranged according to this yarn thickness, from super fine to super bulky weight. And while the specific yarn is listed in every pattern's materials list, you will likely be trying to choose equivalent yarns from your stash to create the projects. Here's how:

Yarn sizes and weights are usually located on the label; but for an accurate test, knit a swatch of stockinette stitch using the recommended needle size, making it at least 4"/[10cm] square.

Count the number of stitches in this 4"/[10cm] swatch and refer to the table on page 10 to determine the yarn's weight.

If you're planning to use several yarns within a single project, take the time to swatch all candidates on the same swatch. This will allow you to see which yarns will drape in a similar fashion and whether they all will have the same "hand" when knitted.

Keep in mind that two or more strands of thin yarns can be combined to create a thicker one for knitting. Refer to the chart on page 12 for details.

Do I Have What It Takes?

Every project requires a specific amount of yarn for completion. The patterns in this book relay this information in yards/[meters]. Check your yarn labels to determine if you have enough. If it's a partial ball, you can physically measure its yardage or weigh it, then check the yarn specifications for that type of yarn (if you know what it is) on the internet and extrapolate the yardage from the weight. (Or just keep your fingers crossed as you knit. You can always simply move to the next color a tad early, if necessary. It might add visual interest to your piece!) To figure out if you have enough yarn to finish a row, keep in mind that the length of yarn required to work a row of stockinette stitch is typically three times the width of the row. Other stitch patterns use more yarn, especially ribs and cables.

So, with your beloved stash now neatly organized, and armed with creative new ideas for using it, let's get knitting! Isn't that why you wanted the yarn to begin with?!

part two

waste not, want not:
No One Will Ever Know These Projects
Were Made from Leftovers!

Once you've sifted through and organized your stash, use
it to knit the following projects. Each pattern is designed
to create a finished and cohesive look with odds and ends.
No one will ever know that you shopped in your stash for
materials!

In this section, you'll find patterns for sweaters, jackets,
fashion accessories, afghans—even a reusable market bag!
(Using leftover yarn to create a reusable shopping bag:
Now *that's* recycling!)

oh, so fine!

five projects using super fine and fine yarns

Is your stash full of fine weight yarn? Knit the projects in this chapter to dwindle it down! Each one uses fingering or sportweight yarn (CYCA categories 1 and 2). These thin yarns lend themselves to small projects, such as an infant's first jacket (Keiki Baby Kimono, page 45) or warm fashion accessories that are perfect under a winter coat, such as Mona's Little Bias Scarf (page 41) and the Fire and Ice Cozy Cowl (page 39). Lightweight and easy to tuck into your knitting bag, these projects are great for knitting on the go. Bonus!

boho bangles

Whether worn individually or stacked together, these bracelets are a great use of scrap yarn. And check out the DIY box on page 32 to learn how to design your own.

SKILL LEVEL
Advanced Beginner

SIZE
Each bangle will fit an adult woman's wrist

FINISHED MEASUREMENTS
The Aztec Bangle and the Dots Bangle each measure 1" [3cm] wide; the Cable Bangle measures 2³/₄" [7cm] wide

MATERIALS
- Fine/Sportweight yarn [2]
  - 9 yd/[8.5m] of each of 4 colors for the Aztec Bangle
  - 17 yd/[16m] of each of 2 colors for the Dots Bangle
  - 30 yd/[27.5m] for the Cable Bangle
- Size 3 [3.25mm] knitting needles, or size needed to obtain gauge
- 1 cable needle
- 3 purchased bangle bracelets, two 1¹/₄" [3cm] wide and one 2³/₄" [7cm] wide
- Blunt-end yarn needle

The sample projects use Louet North America's Gems Fine/Sportweight (2-fine/sportweight; 100% superwash merino wool; each approximately 3¹/₂oz/ [100g] and 225 yd/[205.5m]): #47 Terra Cotta (A), #53 Caribou (B), #51 Pink Panther (C), and #30 Cream (D)

GAUGE
31 stitches and 32 rows = 4"/[10cm] in stranded stockinette stitch.
To save time, take time to check gauge.

NOTE
- For the colorwork in the charts, use the stranded technique (pages 133–134).

STITCH PATTERNS
Aztec Pattern (multiple of 4 stitches) See chart.

Dots Pattern (over 16 stitches) See chart.

Cable Pattern (over 19 stitches) See chart.

Alternative Colorway 1   Alternative Colorway 2

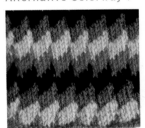 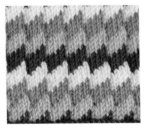

Louet North America's *Gems Fine/ Sportweight:* A = #45 Violet, B = #48 Aqua, C = #26 Crabapple, and D = #22 Black

A = #39 Fern Green, B = #48 Aqua, C = #54 Teal, and D = #05 Goldilocks

AZTEC BANGLE

With A, cast on 16 stitches.

Begin the Aztec Pattern, and work even until the piece measures approximately 10"/[25.5cm] from the beginning.

Bind off, leaving a 36"/[91.5cm] tail.

DOTS BANGLE

With B, cast on 16 stitches.

Begin the Dots Pattern, and work even until the piece measures approximately 10"/[25.5cm] from the beginning.

Bind off, leaving a 36"/[91.5cm] tail.

CABLE BANGLE

With A, cast on 19 stitches.

Begin the Cable Pattern, and work even until the piece measures approximately 10"/[25.5cm] from the beginning.

Bind off, leaving a 36"/[91.5cm] tail.

FINISHING

Darn in all remaining yarn tails (page 135).

Sew the cast-on edge to the bound-off edge.

Place the knitted fabric on top of the appropriate bangle, and sew the long side seam, enclosing the bangle inside the fabric.

Fasten off and darn in the remaining yarn tail.

scrap happy

It would be easy to create the two multicolored bangles using even smaller bits of yarn. For the Aztec Bangle, just add a new color each time the colors change (every four rows); for the Dots Bangle, use a different contrast color for the circular motifs, changing colors on Row 1 and on Row 4.

DIY   switch it up!

It's easy—and fun!—to design your own bangle covers. Simply knit a swatch in a stitch pattern you love, and count the number of stitches per inch. Then, carefully measure the distance around the side of your bracelet (all the way around so it will be lined as well as covered), and multiply this number by your stitch gauge, allowing for a little stretch. Add one selvedge stitch to each side for seaming, and happily cast on! You could even knit a bunch out of leftover yarn to coordinate with all your handmade sweaters. . . .

Aztec Pattern

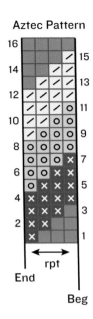

rpt

End

Beg

Dots Pattern

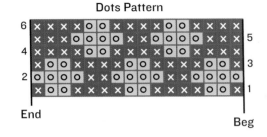

End

Beg

Cable Pattern

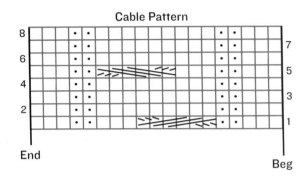

End

Beg

Color Key

⬛ = A

☒ = B

⊙ = C

⧄ = D

Stitch Key

☐ = K on RS; p on WS

• = P on RS; k on WS

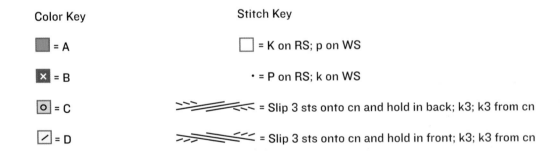 = Slip 3 sts onto cn and hold in back; k3; k3 from cn

= Slip 3 sts onto cn and hold in front; k3; k3 from cn

greenmarket bag

Here's a definite win-win! Knit this eco-friendly shopping bag and help save the planet while using up your stash. Its base is worked with the yarn doubled for extra stability, and the openwork pattern on its body will expand nicely to accommodate all your goodies.

SKILL LEVEL
Intermediate

SIZE
One size

FINISHED MEASUREMENTS
Width: 11"/[28cm]
Height: 12"/[30.5cm] (excluding strap)
Depth: 4"/[10cm]

MATERIALS
- Fine/sportweight yarn 🔲2🔲
  - 325 yd/[297.5m] in the main color (A)
  - 32 yd/[29.5m] in each of 5 contrasting colors (B, C, D, E, and F)
- Size 6 [4mm] knitting needles, or size needed to obtain gauge
- Size 6 [4mm] circular knitting needle, 24"/[60cm] long, or size needed to obtain gauge
- Size 6 [4mm] double-pointed knitting needles (set of 4), or size needed to obtain gauge
- 1 stitch marker
- 2 stitch holders
- Blunt-end yarn needle

The sample project uses Louet North America's Euroflax Fine/Sportweight (2-fine; 100% linen; each approximately 3½ oz/[100g] and 270 yd/[247m]): #55 Willow (A), #30 Cream (B), #51 Pink Panther (C), #05 Goldilocks (D), #47 Terra Cotta (E), and #67 Sea Foam (F)

GAUGE
18 stitches and 36 rows = 4"/[10cm] in garter stitch with 2 strands of yarn held together.
13 stitches and 36 rounds = 4"/[10cm] in the Openwork Pattern using 1 strand of yarn.
To save time, take time to check gauge.

NOTES
- The main color is A; all other colors (B, C, D, E, and F) are contrast colors.
- To increase for the base of the bag, k1, M1 knitwise (page 131), knit across until 1 stitch remains in the row, ending the row with M1 knitwise, k1.
- To decrease for the base of bag, k1, ssk (page 132), knit across until 3 stitches remain in the row, ending the row with k2tog, k1.

STITCH PATTERNS

Garter Stitch (any number of stitches)
ROW 1 (RS): Knit across.
PATTERN ROW: As Row 1.

Openwork Pattern (multiple of 2 sts)
ROUND 1 (RS): With a contrast color, knit around.
ROUND 2: With a contrast color, *p2tog, yarn over; repeat from the * around.
ROUND 3: With A, knit around.
ROUND 4: With A, purl around.
Repeat Rounds 1–4 for the pattern.

Stripe Pattern
Work *2 rounds with B, 2 rounds with A, 2 rounds with C, 2 rounds with A, 2 rounds with D, 2 rounds with A, 2 rounds with E, 2 rounds with A, 2 rounds with F, 2 rounds with A; repeat from the * for the pattern.

Alternative Colorway 1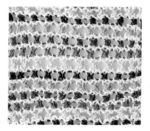

Alternative Colorway 2

Louet North America's _Euroflax Fine/ Sportweight_: A = #30 Cream, B = #44 Sandalwood, C = #43 Pewter, D = #01 Champagne, E = #53 Caribou, and F = #36 Natural

A = #36 Natural, B = #16 Navy, C = #45 Violet, D = #57 French Blue, E = #14 Caribbean Blue, and F = #48 Aqua

BAG

Base of Bag

With 2 strands of A held together, cast on 18 stitches.

Begin in garter stitch, and increase 1 stitch at each side (see Notes) every other row 4 times—26 stitches.

Continue even until the piece measures approximately 8³⁄₄"/ [22cm] from the beginning, ending after a wrong-side row.

Decrease 1 stitch at each side (see Notes) every other row 4 times—18 stitches remain.

Bind off. _Do not fasten off._

Begin Body of Bag

With the right side facing, circular needle, and one strand of A, working along the base piece of the bag, pick up and knit 14 stitches along the top short edge, 35 stitches along one long side edge, 14 stitches along the lower edge, and 35 stitches along the other long edge—98 stitches total.

Join, placing a marker for the beginning of the round.

Begin the Openwork Pattern in the Stripe Pattern, and work even until the piece measures approximately 14"/[35.5cm] from the base, ending after Round 3 of the pattern worked in A.

NEXT ROW (RS): Bind off 14 stitches, p35, bind off 14 stitches, p35.

Shape Strap

ROW 1 (RS): With a contrast color, k2tog, knit across until 2 stitches remain in the row, ending the row with k2tog—33 stitches. Slip the remaining 35 stitches onto a holder.

ROW 2: With the contrast color, k1, *yarn over, k2tog; repeat from the * across.

ROWS 3 AND 4: With A, knit across. Using only A, repeat the last 4 rows 13 more times—7 stitches remain.

Continue even in the pattern as established until this strap measures approximately 12"/ [30.5cm] from the beginning, ending after Row 4 of the pattern. Do not bind off. Slip these 7 stitches onto a holder.

FOR THE SECOND SIDE OF THE STRAP, with the right side facing and the same contrast color used to begin shaping the other side of the strap, work across the 35 stitches from the first holder as follows: K2tog, knit across until 2 stitches remain in the row, ending the row with k2tog—33 stitches.

Complete this side of the strap the same way as the other side.

To connect the 2 sides of the strap together, with both sets of 7 stitches on separate double-pointed needles and with their right sides together, use A and work the three-needle bind-off (page 134).

FINISHING
Darn in all remaining yarn tails (page 135).

scrap happy

Each two-row stripe uses approximately 4½ yd/[4m] of yarn.

Stretching Should Occur in the Gym, Not While Running Errands

To reinforce the strap, measure the width and length of strap from the top of the lining on one side of the bag to the top of the lining on the other side. Add ¼"/[1.5cm] to each dimension. Cut a piece of lining fabric and a piece of interfacing to those dimensions and fuse them together according to the manufacturer's instructions. Use an iron to press under ¼"/[1cm] on all sides for the hems. Pin the lining to the wrong side of strap and sew it down all around, sewing ends to the bag lining.

fire and ice cozy cowl

Light as air, this little cowl doubles as a fashion accessory and winter warmer. Choose a cohesive color palette as shown in the photo or make yours completely scrappy—it will go with more outfits that way. Bonus!

SKILL LEVEL
Intermediate

SIZE
One size

FINISHED MEASUREMENTS
Circumference: 24½"/[62cm]
Depth: 20"/[51cm]

MATERIALS
- Fine sportweight yarn 🄸2
  - 92 yd/[84m] in each of 7 colors
- Size 4 [3.5 mm] circular knitting needle, 16"/[40.5 cm] long, or size needed to obtain gauge
- 1 stitch marker
- Blunt-end yarn needle

The sample project uses Rowan Yarn's Kidsilk Haze (2-fine/sportweight; 70% super kid mohair/30% silk; each approximately 1 oz/[25g] and 229 yd/[210m]): #643 Flower (A), #583 Blushes (B), #595 Liqueur (C), #600 Dewberry (D), #580 Grace (E), #641 Blackcurrant (F), and #606 Candy Girl (G)

GAUGE
27 stitches and 32 rounds = 4"/[10cm] in the Lace Pattern.
To save time, take time to check gauge.

STITCH PATTERNS
Garter Stitch (any number of stitches)
ROUND 1 (RS): Knit.
ROUND 2: Purl.
Repeat Rounds 1 and 2 for the pattern.

Lace Pattern (multiple of 11 stitches)
See chart.

Stripe Pattern
Work *4 rounds with B, 4 rounds with C, 4 rounds with D, 4 rounds with E, 4 rounds with F, 4 rounds with G, 4 rounds with A; repeat from the * for the pattern.

Alternative Colorway 1

Rowan Yarn's *Kidsilk Haze*: A = #606 Candy Girl, B = #645 Garden, C = #583 Blushes, D = #597 Jelly, E = #596 Marmalade, F = #643 Flower, and G = #581 Meadow

Alternative Colorway 2

A = #629 Fern, B = #649 Brick, C = #595 Liqueur, D = #597 Jelly, E = #627 Blood, F = #644 Ember, and G = #628 Cocoa

COWL

With A, cast on 165 stitches.

Place a marker for the beginning of the round. Join, being careful not to twist the stitches on the needle.

Work 4 rounds of garter stitch.

Change to B, begin the Lace Pattern in the Stripe Pattern, and work even until the piece measures approximately 19 3/4"/[50cm] from the beginning, ending after 4 rounds of any color.

Change to A, and work 4 rounds of garter stitch.

Bind off.

FINISHING

Darn in all remaining yarn tails (page 135).

Block the piece to the finished measurements (page 135).

scrap happy

Each 4-round stripe uses approximately 10½ yd/[26.5m] of yarn.

Lace Pattern

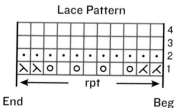

rpt

End   Beg

Stitch Key

☐ = K

· = P

o = Yarn over

ㅅ = K2tog

ㅅ = Ssk

mona's little bias scarf

mona's little bias scarf

The construction of this little scarf makes the ongoing stripes appear to be diagonal. Create the magic ball of yarn ahead of time for effortless knitting. I bet you'll want to keep adding "just one more row" to see the color pattern develop!

SKILL LEVEL
Advanced Beginner

SIZE
One size

FINISHED MEASUREMENTS
Width: 4½"/[11.5cm]
Length: 58"/[147.5cm]

MATERIALS
- Fine/sportweight yarn 〔2〕
  – 275 yd/[251.5m] total in assorted colors
- Size 3 [3.25mm] knitting needles, or size needed to obtain gauge
- Blunt-end yarn needle

The sample project uses a magic ball created with Russian joins (page 22) made with various colors of Blue Sky Alpacas' Sportweight and Melange (2-fine; 100% baby alpaca; each approximately 1¾ oz/[50g] and 110 yd/[100m]): #511 Red (A), #810 Cotton Candy (B), #518 Scarlet (C), #542 Currant (D), #538 Hibiscus (E), #813 Pomegranate (F), #521 Tangerine (G), #811 Bubble Gum (H), #512 Eggplant (I), and #806 Salsa (J).

GAUGE
20 stitches and 40 rows = 4"/[10cm] in garter stitch.
To save time, take time to check gauge.

STITCH PATTERN
Garter Stitch (any number of sts)
PATTERN ROW: Knit across.

Alternative Colorway 1

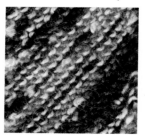

Blue Sky Alpacas' *Sportweight and Melange*: A = #501 Natural Dark Brown, B = #505 Natural Taupe, C = #503 Natural Medium Tan, D = #506 Natural Streaky Brown, E = #809 Toasted Almond, F = #802 Pesto, G = #540 Cappuccino, H = #500 Natural White, I = #814 Pumpernickel, and J = #504 Natural Light Tan

Alternative Colorway 2

A = #500 Natural White, B = #524 Nickel, C = #536 Citron, D = #519 Amber, E = #505 Natural Taupe, F = #808 Relish, G = #807 Dijon, H = #504 Natural Light Tan, I = #520 Avocado, and J = #503 Natural Medium Tan

SCARF

With your magic ball of yarn made with the Russian join technique (page 22), cast on 25 stitches.

ROW 1 (RS): K2, yarn over, knit across until 5 stitches remain in the row, ending the row with k3tog, yarn over, k2.

ROW 2: Knit across.

ROWS 3 AND 4: As Rows 1 and 2.

ROW 5: K2 (yarn over, k2tog), 9 times, yarn over, k3tog, yarn over, k2.

ROW 6: As Row 2.

Repeat Rows 1 and 2 until the scarf is approximately 1"/[2.5cm] short of the desired length.

NEXT 2 ROWS: As Rows 5 and 6.

LAST 4 ROWS: As Rows 1 and 2.

Bind off.

FINISHING

Darn in all remaining yarn tails (page 135).

Block the piece to the finished measurements (page 135).

scrap happy

You'd be surprised how forgiving a magic ball project can be. Even seemingly disparate colors create a cohesive color story when used throughout a project in this way— and bits of any length will work!

keiki baby kimono

Make this cute jacket for your favorite Little One. No one will ever guess it sprang from your yarn stash!

SKILL LEVEL
Intermediate

SIZES
Infant's size 6 months (12 months, 18 months, 24 months). Instructions are for the smallest size, with changes for other sizes noted in parentheses as necessary.

FINISHED MEASUREMENTS
Chest (closed): 20 (21, 22, 23)"/[51 (53.5, 56, 58.5) cm]
Length: 10 (10½, 11, 11½)"/[25.5 (26.5, 28, 29) cm]

MATERIALS
- Super fine/fingering weight yarn (1)
  - 105 (115, 130, 140) yd/[96 (105, 119, 128)m] each in A and B
  - 145 (160, 180, 195) yd/[132.5 (146.5, 165, 178.5)m] in C
  - 165 (180, 200, 220) yd/[151 (165, 183, 201)m] in D
  - 65 (70, 80, 85) yd/[59.5 (64, 73, 78)m] in E
  - 25 (25, 30, 30) yd/[23 (23, 27.5, 27.5)m] in F
- Size 2 [2.75mm] knitting needles, or size needed to obtain gauge
- Size 2 [2.75mm] circular knitting needle, 24"/[60cm] long, or size needed to obtain gauge
- Blunt-end yarn needle
- 4 stitch markers
- 1½ yd/[1.5m] ribbon
- Sewing thread to match ribbon
- Sharp sewing needle

The sample project uses Brown Sheep Company's Cotton Fine (*1-super fine/fingering weight; 80% cotton/20% merino wool; each approximately 1¾ oz/ [50g] and 222 yd/[203m]*): #CW844 Celery Leaves (A), #CW915 Majestic Orchid (B), #CW210 Tea Rose (C), #CW560 My Blue Heaven (D), #CW343 Sunflower Gold (E), and #CW767 Hawaiian Sky (F)

GAUGE
32 stitches and 39 rows = 4"/[10cm] in the stranded stockinette stitch.
To save time, take time to check gauge.

NOTES
- For the colorwork in the charts, use stranded technique (pages 133–134).
- For a fully fashioned decrease at the beginning of a row: On right-side rows, k1, ssk (page 132), continue the pattern as established across to end the row; on wrong-side rows, p1, p2tog (page 131), continue the pattern as established across to end the row.
- For a fully fashioned decrease at the end of a row: On right-side rows, work the pattern as established across until 3 stitches remain in the row, ending the row with k2tog (page 130), k1; on wrong-side rows, work the pattern as established across until 3 stitches remain in the row, ending the row with ssp (page 132), p1.
- To increase: K1, M1 knitwise (page 131), work across until 1 stitch remains in the row, ending the row with M1 knitwise, k1.
- For sweater assembly, refer to the illustration for drop-shoulder construction on page 136.

STITCH PATTERNS

Stripes and Dots Pattern (multiple of 6 + 1 stitches)
See chart.

**Zigzag Pattern for Left Front
(multiple of 6 + 1 stitches)**
See chart.

**Zigzag Pattern for Right Front
(multiple of 6 + 1 stitches)**
See chart.

Alternative Colorway 1

**Brown Sheep Company's *Cotton
Fine*:** A = #CW343 Sunflower Gold,
B = #CW201 Barn Red, C = #CW765
Blue Paradise, D = #CW100 Cotton
Ball, E = #CW840 Lime Light, and F =
#CW310 Wild Orange

Alternative Colorway 2

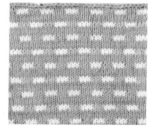

A = #CW620 Banana, B = #CW690
Alpine Lilac, C = #CW365 Peridot,
D = #CW210 Tea Rose, E = #CW610
Nymph, and F = #CW100 Cotton
Ball

BACK

With C, cast on 80 (84, 88, 92) stitches.

Begin the Stripes and Dots Pattern, and work even until the piece measures approximately 10 (10½, 11, 11½)"/[25.5 (26.5, 28, 29) cm] from the beginning, ending after a wrong-side row.

Bind off.

RIGHT FRONT

With C, cast on 67 (73, 79, 79) stitches.

Begin the Zigzag Pattern for Right Front, and work even until the piece measures approximately 3 (3½, 3½, 4)"/[7.5 (9, 9, 10)cm] from the beginning, ending after a wrong-side row.

Shape Neck

Work fully fashioned decreases (see Notes) at the beginning of the next row and at the neck edge every row 21 (29, 31, 27) more times, then every other row 23 (19, 21, 23) times—22 (24, 26, 28) stitches remain.

Bind off.

LEFT FRONT

With D, cast on 67 (73, 79, 79) stitches.

Begin the Zigzag Pattern for Left Front, and work even until the piece measures approximately 3 (3½, 3½, 4)"/[7.5 (9, 9, 10)cm] from the beginning, ending after a wrong-side row.

Shape Neck

Work fully fashioned decreases (see Notes) at the end of the next row and at the neck edge every row 21 (29, 31, 27) more times, then every other row 23 (19, 21, 23) times—22 (24, 26, 28) stitches remain.

Bind off.

SLEEVE (MAKE 2)

With C, cast on 55 (55, 61, 61) stitches.

Begin the Stripes and Dots Pattern, and work fully fashioned increases (see Notes) at each side every other row 0 (3, 0, 0) times, every fourth row 9 (8, 10, 7) times, then every sixth row 0 (0, 0, 3) times, working new stitches into the pattern as they accumulate—73 (77, 81, 81) stitches.

Continue even until the sleeve measures approximately 4¾ (5, 5 ¼, 5¾)"/[12 (12.5, 13.5, 14.5)cm] from the beginning, ending after a wrong-side row.

Bind off.

FINISHING

Darn in all remaining yarn tails (page 135).

Block all pieces to the finished measurements (page 135).

Sew the shoulder seams.

Place markers 4½ (4¾, 5, 5)"/[11.5 (12, 12.5, 12.5)cm] down from the shoulders on fronts and back.

Set in the sleeves between the markers.

Sleeve Edging

With right side facing and D, pick up and knit 54 (54, 60, 60) stitches along the lower edge of the sleeve.

NEXT ROW (WS): Knit across.
NEXT ROW: Purl across.
NEXT ROW: Knit as you bind off.

Repeat for the second sleeve.

Sew the side and sleeve seams.

scrap happy

If you have smaller amounts of yarn than those called for in the pattern, make each zigzag stripe a different color on the fronts.

DIY | *button it up!*

For a completely different look, use hidden snap closures instead of ribbon ties.

Front and Neckline Edging

With the right side facing, circular needle, and D, begin at the lower Right Front edge and pick up and knit 26 (30, 30, 34) stitches along the flat section of the Right Front, place a marker, pick up and knit 77 (79, 81, 85) stitches along the Right Front neck opening, pick up and knit 38 stitches along the back of the neck, pick up and knit 77 (79, 81, 85) stitches along the Left Front neck opening, place a marker, pick up and knit 26 (30, 30, 34) stitches along the flat section of Left Front—244 (256, 260, 276) stitches.

NEXT ROW (WS): Knit across to the marker, slip the marker, M1 knitwise, knit across to the next marker, M1 knitwise, slip the marker, knit across to end the row.
NEXT ROW: Purl across.
NEXT ROW: Bind off as you knit across to the first marker, M1 knitwise, bind off as you knit across to the next marker, M1 knitwise, bind off as you knit across to end the row.

Lower Body Edging

With the right side facing, circular needle, and D, pick up and knit 214 (230, 246, 250) stitches along the lower edge of Left Front, Back, and Right Front.

Complete the same as the sleeve edging.

Ribbon Ties

Cut the ribbon into four 12"/ [30.5cm] pieces.

Sew a piece of ribbon to both the Right and Left Fronts just below the beginning of the neck shaping.

Overlap the fronts, and place markers on the inside of the Left Front and on the outside of the Right Front, corresponding with the positions of the existing ties. Sew the other 2 pieces of ribbon at the marked locations.

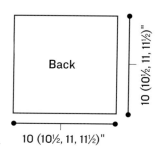

Back

10 (10½, 11, 11½)"

10 (10½, 11, 11½)"

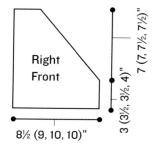

Right Front

8½ (9, 10, 10)"

3 (3½, 3½, 4)"

7 (7, 7½, 7½)"

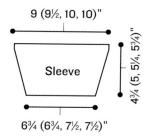

9 (9½, 10, 10)"

Sleeve

6¾ (6¾, 7½, 7½)"

4¾ (5, 5¼, 5¾)"

Zigzag Pattern for Left Front

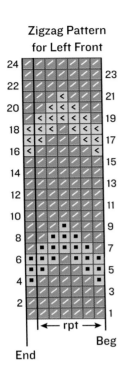

Zigzag Pattern for Right Front

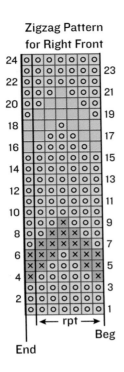

Stripes and Dots Pattern

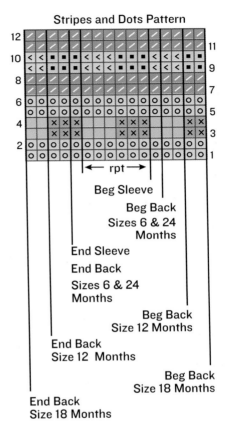

Beg Sleeve

Beg Back
Sizes 6 & 24
Months

End Sleeve

End Back
Sizes 6 & 24
Months

Beg Back
Size 12 Months

End Back
Size 12 Months

Beg Back
Size 18 Months

End Back
Size 18 Months

Color Key

☐ = A

☒ = B

▣ = C

◩ = D

◁ = E

▪ = F

Stitch Key

☐ = K on RS; p on WS

lightweight but still big on style

3

five projects using DK weight yarns

If your yarn stash is loaded with lightweight yarns, use the following patterns to whittle it away. Each project calls for DK weight yarn (CYCA category 3), perfect for menswear (Sea of Blue, on page 71), kidswear (Sporty Stripes, page 61), and other items. And don't forget that two strands of fine yarn held together while knitting will also work nicely for projects calling for lightweight yarn! Waste not, want not.

harlequin

Use as many colors as you like to create this intarsia project or choose several shades of the same hue as seen in the sample bag.

SKILL LEVEL
Intermediate

SIZES
One size

FINISHED MEASUREMENTS
Width: 12"/[30.5cm]
Length: 8½"/[21.5cm]

MATERIALS
- Light/DK weight yarn (3)
  - 424 yd/[388m] in the main color (B)
  - 107 yd/[98m] in each of 3 contrast colors (A, C, and D)
- Size 5 [3.75mm] knitting needles, or size needed to obtain gauge
- Size 3 [3.25mm] knitting needles
- Size C/2 [2.75mm] crochet hook
- Blunt-end yarn needle
- ½ yd/[.5m] coordinating fabric for lining]
- ½ yd/[.5m] iron-on interfacing for added stability (optional)
- Pins
- Matching sewing thread
- Sharp sewing needle

The sample project uses Brown Sheep Company's Nature Spun Sport (3-light/DK weight; 100% wool; each approximately 1¾ oz/[50g] and 184 yd/[168m]): #207 Alpine Violet (A), #N62 Amethyst (B), #N65 Sapphire (C), and #N60 Purple Splendor (D)

GAUGE
24 stitches and 28 rows = 4"/[10cm] in stockinette stitch with the larger needles.
To save time, take time to check gauge.

NOTE
- Use the intarsia technique (pages 129–130) for the colorwork.

STITCH PATTERNS
Harlequin Pattern (multiple of 24 + 1 stitches)
See the chart.

Strap Pattern (multiple of 2 + 1 stitches)
ROW 1 (RS): K1, *slip the next stitch with the yarn in back, k1; repeat from the * to the end of the row.
ROW 2: Knit across.
Repeat Rows 1 and 2 for the pattern.

Alternative Colorway 1

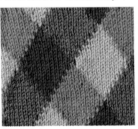

Brown Sheep Company's *Nature Spun Sport:* A = #N56 Meadow Green, B = #522 Nervous Green, C = #155 Bamboo, and D = #103 Deep Sea

Alternative Colorway 2

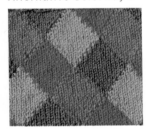

A = #N17 French Clay, B = #308 Sunburst Gold, C = #522 Nervous Green, and D = #105 Bougainvillea

BACK

With the larger needles and C, cast on 73 stitches.

Begin the Harlequin Pattern and work even until the piece measures approximately 19"/[48.5cm] from the beginning, ending after Row 36 of the pattern.

Bind off with B.

FRONT

Work the same as Back until the piece measures approximately 8½"/[21.5cm] from the beginning, ending after Row 12 of the pattern.

Bind off with B.

STRAP/GUSSET

With the smaller needles and B, cast on 19 stitches.

Begin the Strap Pattern, and work even until the piece measures approx 66"/[167.5cm] from the beginning, ending after a wrong-side row.

Bind off in pattern.

Reinforce the strap (page 37).

FINISHING

Darn in all remaining yarn tails (page 135).

Block all pieces to the finished measurements (page 135).

Lining

Cut the lining to fit the bag, including the flap.

(Optional: Cut the iron-on interface to fit the lining, including the flap.

Follow manufacturer's instructions to fuse the interface to the wrong side of the lining fabric.)

With the right side facing, sew the cast-on and bind-off edges of the Strap/Gusset together.

With the right side facing and centering the Strap/Gusset seam at the center bottom of the Front, sew one side of the Strap/Gusset to the Front. Sew the other side of the Strap/Gusset to the Back, leaving 12"/[30.5cm] unsewn for the top flap.

Sew the lining into place, folding ¼"/[1cm] hems to the wrong side.

Edging

With the right side facing, the crochet hook, and B, attach the yarn with a slip stitch to the edge of the top flap and chain 1. Work 180 single crochet stitches evenly spaced along the entire edge of the flap. Chain 1. *Do not turn.*

NEXT ROW: Work one row of reverse single crochet along the edge of the flap, working 1 stitch into each stitch of the previous row. Fasten off.

Work the edging along the upper edge of the Front same as for the flap, working 72 single crochet stitches.

Harlequin Pattern

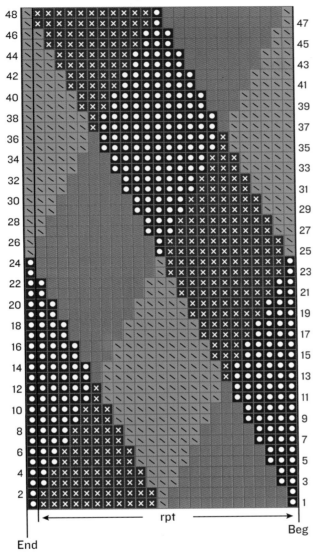

Rows (left side, top to bottom): 48, 46, 44, 42, 40, 38, 36, 34, 32, 30, 28, 26, 24, 22, 20, 18, 16, 14, 12, 10, 8, 6, 4, 2

Rows (right side, top to bottom): 47, 45, 43, 41, 39, 37, 35, 33, 31, 29, 27, 25, 23, 21, 19, 17, 15, 13, 11, 9, 7, 5, 3, 1

← rpt →

End   Beg

scrap happy

Each geometric motif uses approximately 3 yd/[3m] of yarn.

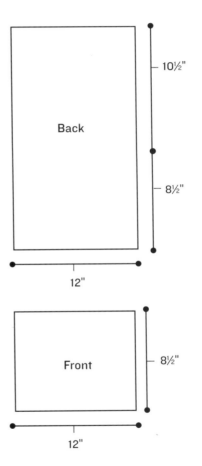

Back — 10½" / 8½"

12"

Front — 8½"

12"

Color Key

▨ = A

☒ = B

◉ = C

◪ = D

Stitch Key

☐ = K on RS; p on WS

toasty

Warm someone's heart as well as his or her hands with these quick-to-stitch mittens.

SKILL LEVEL
Intermediate

SIZES
Average Woman's (Man's) hands. Instructions are for the smaller size, with changes for the other size noted in parentheses as necessary.

FINISHED MEASUREMENTS
Palm Circumference: 8 (9½)"/[20.5 (24)cm]
Length: 11 (12½)"/[28 (32)cm]

MATERIALS
- Light/DK weight yarn (3)
  - 84 (107) yd/[77 (98)m] in the ribbing color (A)
  - 13 (17) yd/[12 (15.5)m] in B
  - 59 (68) yd/[54 (62)m] in C
  - 22 (27) yd/[20 (25)m] in D
  - 12 (16) yd/[11 (14.5)m] in E
- Sizes 4 and 6 [3.5 and 4mm] double-pointed knitting needles (set of 4), or size needed to obtain gauge
- 3 stitch markers, 1 in a contrasting color for the beginning of the round
- 1 stitch holder
- Blunt-end yarn needle

The sample project uses Aurora Yarn's/Ornaghi Filati's Merino Kind (3-light/DK weight; 100% superwash merino wool; each approximately 1¾ oz/[50g] and 137 yd/[125]): Dark Charcoal #080 (A), Cream #177 (B), Pale Gray #082 (C), Black #021 (D), and Mid Gray #081 (E)

GAUGE
22 stitches and 28 rounds = 4"/[10cm] in stockinette stitch worked in the round with larger needles.
To save time, take time to check gauge.

NOTES
- To decrease, use the k2tog technique (page 130).
- For ease in finishing, do not cut the yarn after each stripe; instead, carry it loosely up the wrong side of the fabric until it is needed again.

STITCH PATTERNS
***Rib Pattern** (multiple of 2 stitches)*
PATTERN ROUND (RS): *K1, p1; repeat from the * around.

***Stockinette Stitch Worked in the Round** (any number of stitches)*
PATTERN ROUND (RS): Knit around.

Stripe Pattern
Work *1 round with B, 5 rounds with C, 2 rounds with D, 1 round with E, 3 rounds with A; repeat from the * for the pattern.

Alternative Colorway 1

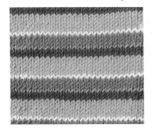

Aurora **Yarn's/Ornaghi Filati's**
Merino Kind: A = #986 Tangerine, B = #026 Pale Pink, C = #034 Peach, D = #711 Fuchsia, and E = #207 Rose

Alternative Colorway 2

A = #940 Gray Taupe, B = #736 Light Terracotta, C = #970 Seaglass, D = #905 Terracotta, and E = #020 Crème

MITTEN
Cuff

With the smaller double-pointed needles and A, cast on 42 (50) stitches. Place a marker for the beginning of the round. Join, being careful not to twist the stitches on the needles.

Begin the Rib Pattern, and work even until the piece measures approximately 3¼ (4)"/[9 (10)cm] from the beginning.

Change to the larger double-pointed needles, begin in stockinette stitch, worked in the round in the Stripe Pattern for 6 (10) rounds.

Place additional markers after the first stitch and before the last stitch of the round.

Begin the Thumb Gore

NEXT ROUND (INCREASE ROUND): Knit to the first marker, M1 knitwise, slip the marker, work to the next marker, slip the marker, M1 knitwise, knit to end the round—44 (52) stitches.

Repeat the Increase Round every other round 4 (6) more times, then every fourth round once—54 (66) stitches with 14 (18) thumb stitches between the markers.

Knit one more round, ending when you reach the second marker.

Separate the Thumb from the Hand

Remove the marker and slip the 14 (18) stitches between markers onto a holder or piece of scrap yarn; using the working yarn, cast on 2 stitches; place a marker for the new beginning of the round; then, using the next color in the stripe sequence, cast on 2 stitches and complete the round—44 (52) stitches.

Continue even in the patterns as established until the piece measures approximately 10 (11½)"/ [25.5 (29)cm] from the beginning; decrease 4 stitches evenly spaced along the last round—40 (48) stitches remain.

Decrease for the Tip

NEXT ROUND: *K2, k2tog; repeat from the * around—30 (36) stitches remain.

Work even in the patterns for 2 (3) rounds.

NEXT ROUND: *K1, k2tog; repeat from the * around—20 (24) stitches remain.

Work even in the patterns for 2 (3) rounds.

NEXT ROUND: *K2tog; repeat from the * around—10 (12) stitches remain.

Break the yarn, leaving a 6"/[15cm] tail. Thread the tail through the remaining stitches and pull it tight to secure. Fasten off.

THUMB

Slip the 14 (18) stitches from the holder onto 2 double-pointed needles.

Using the appropriate color in the established Stripe Pattern and a third double-pointed needle, pick up and knit 4 stitches along the cast-on at thumb—18 (22) stitches.

Knit across first 7 (9) stitches of thumb. This is now the beginning of the round.

Distribute the stitches evenly over the 3 double-pointed needles. Change color, if necessary, to maintain the Stripe Pattern.

DIY | *easy does it!*

Want solid-colored mittens instead? No problem. One pair of these mittens uses approximately 190 (235) yd/[174 (215)m] of yarn.

 *scrap happy*

Each round of the palm uses approximately 1 yd/[1m] of yarn.

Continue even in the patterns as established for 2½ (2¾)"/[6.5 (7)]cm above the thumb cast-on stitches; decrease 0 (1) stitch at the beginning of the last round—18 (21) stitches remain.

NEXT ROUND: *K1, k2tog; repeat from the * around—12 (14) stitches remain.

NEXT ROUND: *K2tog; repeat from the * around—6 (7) stitches remain.

Break the yarn, leaving a 6"/[15cm] tail. Thread the tail through the remaining stitches and pull it tight to secure. Fasten off.

FINISHING

Darn in all remaining yarn tails (page 135).

Block all pieces to the finished measurements (page 135).

sporty stripes

Varying stripes and simple rolled edges make this design as fun to knit as it will be to wear. See the DIY box on page 66 for suggestions on making it your own.

SKILL LEVEL
Advanced Beginner

SIZES
Child's 2 (4, 6, 8, 10). Instructions are for the smallest size, with changes for the other sizes noted in parentheses as necessary.

FINISHED MEASUREMENTS
Chest: 26 (28, 31, 33, 35)"/[66 (71, 79, 84, 89)cm]
Length (*includes one-half of the top of the sleeve and the rolled edge*): 14¾ (15¼, 17¾, 20, 21½)"/[37.5 (39, 45, 51, 54.5)cm]

MATERIALS
- Light/DK weight yarn (3)
  - 165 (190, 240, 280, 325) yd/[151 (174, 219.5, 256, 297)m] in A
  - 70 (85, 110, 130, 145) yd/[64 (78, 100.5, 119, 132.5)m] in B
  - 115 (140, 180, 215, 245) yd/[105 (128, 164.5, 196.5, 224)m] in C
  - 70 (85, 110 130, 145) yd/[64 (78, 100.5, 119, 132.5)m] each in D and E
- Size 6 [4mm] knitting needles, or size needed to obtain gauge
- Size 6 [4mm] circular knitting needle, 16"/[40cm] long or size needed to obtain gauge
- 1 stitch marker
- Blunt-end yarn needle

The sample project uses Plymouth Yarn's Jeannee DK (3-light/DK weight yarn; 51% cotton/49% acrylic; each approximately 1¾ oz [50g] and 136 yd/[124.5m]) in #54 Zinnia (A), #55 Lime (B), #25 Petunia Pink (C), #53 Tangerine (D), and #56 Sunshine (E)

GAUGE
22 stitches and 32 rows = 4"/[10cm] in stockinette stitch with the larger needles.
To save time, take time to check gauge.

NOTES
- Row gauge is crucial for raglan garments, so be sure to check both your stitch and your row gauge.
- To ensure that all the stripes match during the raglan shaping, be sure to begin the shaping on the same row of the stripe pattern for all pieces.
- The lower edge of sweater pieces will roll; all measurements include this rolled edge.
- For fully fashioned increases on right-side rows, k2, M1 knitwise (page 131), work across until 2 stitches remain, ending row with M1 knitwise, k2.
- For fully fashioned decreases: On right-side rows, k2, ssk, work across in the pattern as established until 4 stitches remain, ending the row with k2tog, k2; on wrong-side rows, p2, p2tog, work across in the pattern as established until 4 stitches remain, ending the row with ssp, p2.
- For sweater assembly, refer to the illustration for raglan construction on page 136.

STITCH PATTERNS

Stockinette Stitch (any number of stitches)
ROW 1 (RS): Knit across.
ROW 2: Purl across.
Repeat Rows 1 and 2 for the pattern.

Stripe Pattern
Work *2 rows with A, 1 row with B, 4 rows with C, 2 rows with D, 1 row with E, 4 rows with A, 2 rows with B, 1 row with C, 1 row with D, 2 rows with E; repeat from the * for the pattern.

Alternative Colorway 1

Plymouth Yarn's *Jeannee DK*: A = #10 Denim, B = #6 Khaki, C = #21 Sky, D = #32 Chamois, and E = #8 Cream

Alternative Colorway 2

A = #51 Cherry, B = #55 Lime, C = #53 Tangerine, D = #56 Sunshine, and E = #14 White

BACK

With A, cast on 72 (78, 86, 92, 98) stitches.

Begin in stockinette stitch in the Stripe Pattern, and work even until the piece measures approximately 8 (8, 10, 11¾, 13)"/[20.5 (20.5, 25.5, 30, 33)cm] from the beginning. *Make a note which row of Stripe Pattern you ended with.*

Shape Raglan

Bind off 3 (3, 3, 4, 4) stitches at the beginning of the next 2 rows—66 (72, 80, 84, 90) stitches remain.

Work fully fashioned decreases at each side (see Notes) every fourth row 4 (3, 2, 2, 1) times, then every other row 15 (19, 23, 24, 27) times—28 (28, 30, 32, 34) stitches remain.

Bind off.

FRONT

Work the same as the Back until the piece measures approximately 11½ (12, 14½, 16½, 18)"/[29 (30.5, 37, 42, 45.5)cm] from the beginning, ending with a wrong-side row.

Shape Neck

Continue the raglan shaping same as for the back, *and at the same time,* bind off the center 12 (12, 14, 16, 18) stitches for the front neck on the next row.

Working both sides at once with separate yarns, bind off 3 stitches at each neck edge once, bind off 2 stitches at each neck edge once, then decrease 1 stitch at each neck edge every row three times.

Complete the same as for the back.

SLEEVE (MAKE 2)

With A, cast on 40 (42, 44, 44, 46) stitches.

Begin in stockinette stitch in the Stripe Pattern, and work fully fashioned increases at each side (see Notes) every eighth row 5 (2, 4, 8, 12) times, then every tenth row 2 (6, 6, 4, 2) times—54 (58, 64, 68, 74) stitches.

Work even until the piece measures approximately 8 (10½, 12½, 14¼, 15½)"/[20.5 (26.5, 32, 36, 39.5)cm] from the beginning, ending after same row of Stripe Pattern as Front and Back.

Shape Raglan

Bind off 3 (3, 3, 4, 4) stitches at the beginning of the next 2 rows—48 (52, 58, 60, 66) stitches remain.

Work fully fashioned decreases at each side (see Notes) every fourth row 3 (3, 2, 3, 1) times, then every other row 17 (19, 23, 22, 27) times—8 (8, 8, 10, 10) stitches remain.

Bind off.

FINISHING

Darn in all remaining yarn tails (page 135).

Block all pieces to the finished measurements (page 135).

Sew the raglan seams.

Neckband

With the right side facing, using the circular needle and A, pick up and knit 90 (90, 94, 98, 102) stitches evenly spaced along the neckline; place a marker and join. Knit around until neckband measures approximately 1½"/ [4cm], allowing it to roll to the right side. Bind off *very loosely*.

Sew the sleeve and side seams.

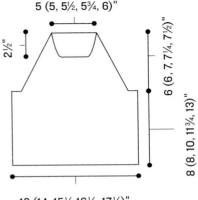

5 (5, 5½, 5¾, 6)"

2½"

6 (6, 7, 7¼, 7½)"

8 (8, 10, 11¾, 13)"

13 (14, 15½, 16½, 17½)"

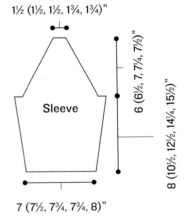

1½ (1½, 1½, 1¾, 1¾)"

6 (6½, 7, 7¼, 7½)"

Sleeve

8 (10½, 12½, 14¼, 15½)"

7 (7½, 7¾, 7¾, 8)"

scrap happy

To use up even smaller bits of yarn, knit the sleeves in random, nonmatching stripes, and make the front and back in a solid, coordinating color.

waves of color

Use your scraps to create this warm, comforting, and luxurious shawl. It is reminiscent of your grandmother's heirloom Old Shale afghan.

SKILL LEVEL
Intermediate

SIZE
One size

FINISHED MEASUREMENTS
Width: 70"/[178m]
Length: 31"/[78.5m]

MATERIALS
- Light/DK weight yarn (3)
  - 76 yd/[69.5m] in each of 3 colors (A, B, and C)
  - 88 yd/[80.5m] in each of 3 colors (D, E, and F)
  - 101 yd/[92.5m] in G
  - 114 yd/[104m] in H, 126 yd/[115m] in I
  - 190 yd/[173.5m] in J
- Size 6 [4mm] circular knitting needle, 36"/[90cm] long, or size needed to obtain gauge
- Stitch markers (optional)
- Blunt-end yarn needle

The sample project uses The Alpaca Yarn Company's Classic Alpaca (3-light/DK weight; 100% superfine alpaca; each approximately 1¾ oz/[50g] and 110 yd/ [100.5m]): #1633 Horizon (A), #1819 Victorian Rose (B), #100 White House (C), #1820 Mixed Berries (D), #1808 Purple Haze (E), #403 Wall Street Flannel (F), #2019 Petal Pink (G), #401 Liberty Gray (H), #2025 Confetti (I), and #1821 Brambleberry (J).

GAUGE
20 stitches and 27 rows = 4"/[10cm] in the Ripple Pattern.
To save time, take time to check gauge.

NOTES
- This shawl is made from the top down; each right-side row is increased by 6 stitches: 2 stitches at each outer edge and 1 stitch on either side of the center stitch.
- The new stitches should be incorporated into the Ripple Pattern as soon as possible. When there are 7 new stitches, begin working them in the Ripple Pattern, working one decrease and its accompanying yarn over; when there are 13 new stitches, work the entire Ripple pattern repeat (see the charts).
- You might find it helpful to use stitch markers to mark the center stitch and to separate the established Ripple Pattern repeats from the sides and center.

STITCH PATTERNS

Ripple Pattern (multiple of 13 stitches)
ROW 1 (RS): *K2tog, k4, yarn over, k1, yarn over, k4, ssk; repeat from the * across.
ROW 2: Purl across.
ROW 3: As Row 1.
ROW 4: *K6, p1, k6; repeat from the * across.
Repeat Rows 1–4 for the pattern, incorporating new stitches into the pattern as soon as possible.

Garter Stitch (any number of stitches)
PATTERN ROW: Knit across.

Stripe Pattern
Work 4 rows *each* with *A, B, C, D, E, F, G, H, I, and J; repeat from the * for the pattern.

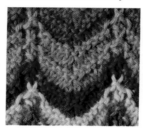 Alternative Colorway 1

 Alternative Colorway 2

The Alpaca Yarn Company's *Classic Alpaca*: A = #2023 Flame, B = #2024 Rosette, C = #2270 In the Buff, D = #2203 Fall Foliage, E = #2408 Citrus, F = #2213 Cayenne, G = #2215 Solar Flare, H = #2250 Burnished Gold, I = #2231 Spiced Brandy, and J = #2201 Sweet Potato

A = #1628 Ocean, B = #1818 Woodland Violet, C = #500 Black, D = #1606 Caribbean Blue, E = #1822 Lavender, F = #1830 Royal Purple, G = #1630 Parrot, H = #1808 Purple Haze, I = #1626 Marine, and J = #1800 Ozark Purple

SHAWL

With A, cast on 3 stitches. Changing colors on the 5th row, then every 4 rows for the Stripe Pattern, follow the right- and left-hand charts through Row 38.

Continue increasing at the sides and center as established, incorporating the new stitches into the Ripple Pattern in the same manner as before until 160 rows (4 stripe sequences) have been worked—481 stitches.

Bind off in the pattern.

FINISHING
Upper Edging

With the same color you ended the main part of the shawl with, with the right side facing, pick up and knit 319 stitches along the upper edge of shawl.

Work 5 rows of garter stitch.

NEXT ROW (WS): Bind off.

Darn in all remaining yarn tails (page 135).

Block the piece to the finished measurements (page 135).

scrap happy

When choosing yarns and colors for this project, keep in mind that each successive stripe will require more yarn than the one before; use yarns you have less of early in the project; save yarns that you have more of for later on.

DIY | *downsize it*

If you'd prefer a shawlette, stop short of the 160 rows. Knit the upper edging in the same color of your last row to tie everything together.

Left Side of Shawl Pattern

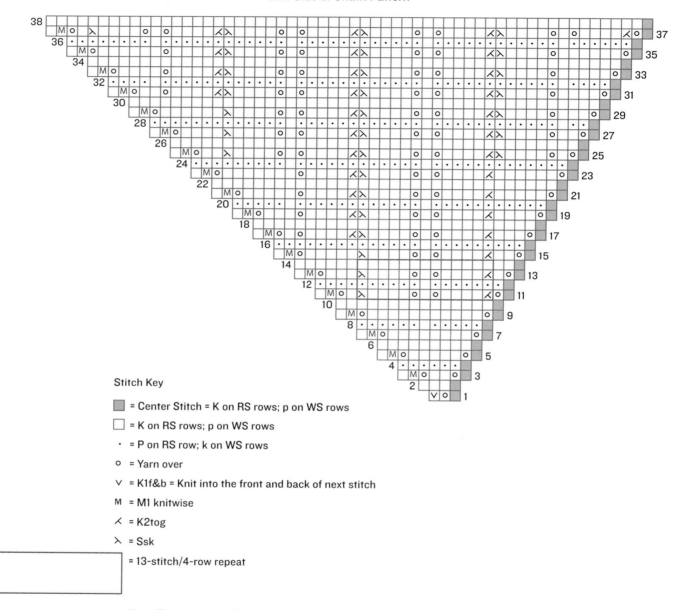

Stitch Key

⬛ = Center Stitch = K on RS rows; p on WS rows

⬜ = K on RS rows; p on WS rows

· = P on RS row; k on WS rows

○ = Yarn over

V = K1f&b = Knit into the front and back of next stitch

M = M1 knitwise

⟋ = K2tog

⟍ = Ssk

▭ = 13-stitch/4-row repeat

Note: The center stitch appears in both left- and right-side charts
but is worked only once per row.

Right Side of Shawl Pattern

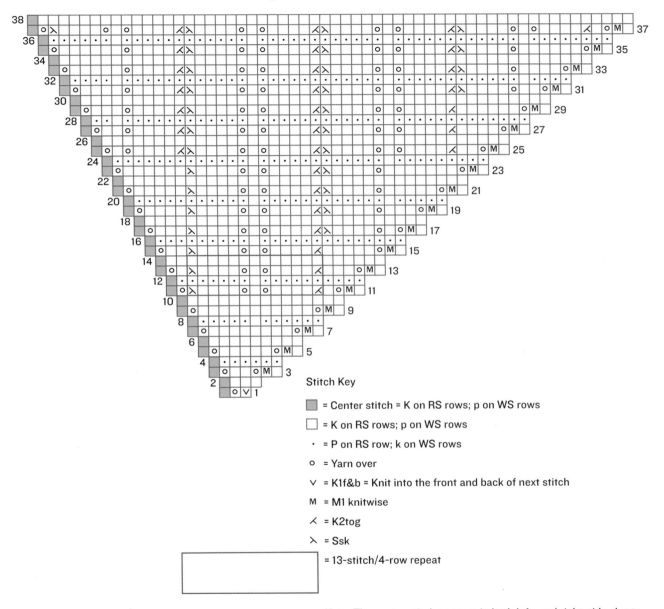

Stitch Key

▨ = Center stitch = K on RS rows; p on WS rows

☐ = K on RS rows; p on WS rows

• = P on RS row; k on WS rows

o = Yarn over

V = K1f&b = Knit into the front and back of next stitch

M = M1 knitwise

⟋ = K2tog

⟍ = Ssk

= 13-stitch/4-row repeat

Note: The center stitch appears in both left- and right-side charts but is worked only once per row.

sea of blue

Combine a million shades of your guy's favorite color to create an intensely personal gift. Be sure to put the Scrap Happy tip to use, cutting off the appropriate yardage for each section of color, to make the knitting easier—and to keep you, the knitter, happier. You'll thank me.

SKILL LEVEL
Intermediate

SIZES
Small (Medium, Large, X-Large, XX-Large).
Instructions are for the smallest size, with changes for other sizes noted in parentheses as necessary.

FINISHED MEASUREMENTS
Chest: 43 (48, 54, 59, 64)"/[109 (122, 137, 150, 162.5)cm]
Length: 26 (26½, 27, 27½, 28)"/[66 (67.5, 68.5, 70, 71)cm]

MATERIALS
- Light/DK weight yarn (**3**)
  - 350 (385, 420, 450, 490) yd/[320 (352, 384, 411.5, 448)m] in the ribbing color (G)
  - 60 (65, 71, 76, 82) yd/[55 (59.5, 65, 69.5, 75)m] in each of 27 contrasting colors (A, B, C, D, E, F, G, H, I, J, K, L, M, N, O, P, Q, R, S, T, U, V, W, X, Y, Z, and AA)
- Size 3 [3.25mm] knitting needles
- Size 4 [3.5mm] knitting needles, or size needed to obtain gauge
- Bobbins (optional)
- Blunt-end yarn needle

The sample project uses Simply Shetland/Jamieson's Double Knitting (3-light/DK weight; 100% Shetland wool; each approximately 1 oz/[25g] and 82 yd/ [75m]): #655 China Blue (A), #710 Gentian (B), #136 Teviot (C), #676 Sapphire (D), #232 Blue Lovat (E), #760 Caspian (F), #684 Cobalt (G), #258 Peacock (H), #175 Twilight (I), #727 Admiral Navy (J), #168 Clyde Blue (K), #150 Atlantic (L), #763 Pacific (M), #726 Prussian Blue (N), #680 Lunar (O), #660 Lagoon (P), #170 Fjord (Q), #730 Dark Navy (R), #134 Blue Danube (S), #700 Royal (T), #135 Surf (U), #1390 Highland Mist (V), #764 Cloud (W), #677 Stonewash (X), #160 Midnight (Y), #1020 Nighthawk (Z), and #750 Petrol (AA)

GAUGE
24 stitches and 32 rows = 4"/[10cm] in stockinette stitch with the larger needles.
To save time, take time to check gauge.

NOTES
- Use the intarsia technique (pages 129–130) for the colorwork on the front, back, and sleeves; use the stranded technique (pages 133–134) for the colorwork on the neckband.
- To decrease, use k2tog (page 130) at the beginning of a row or ssk (page 132) at the end of a row.
- To increase, use the M1 knitwise technique (page 131).
- For sweater assembly, refer to the illustration for square indented construction on page 136.

STITCH PATTERNS

Rib Pattern (multiple of 4 + 2 stitches)
ROW 1 (RS): *K2, p2; repeat from the * across, ending the row with k2.
ROW 2: *P2, k2; repeat from the * across, ending the row with p2.
Repeat Rows 1 and 2 for the pattern.

Stockinette Stitch (any number of stitches)
ROW 1 (RS): Knit across.
ROW 2: Purl across.
Repeat Rows 1 and 2 for the pattern.

Man's Intarsia Pattern, Rows 1–60
See the chart.

Man's Intarsia Pattern, Rows 61–120
See the chart.

Alternative Colorway 1	Alternative Colorway 2

Simply Shetland/Jamieson's *Double Knitting*. A = #429 Old Gold, B = #187 Sunrise, C = #234 Pine, D = #462 Ginger, E = #595 Maroon, F = #410 Cornfield, G = #293 Port Wine, H = #577 Chestnut, I = #1160 Scotch Broom, J = #815 Ivy, K= #1190 Burnt Umber, L = #147 Moss, M = #788 Leaf, N = #235 Grouse, O = #879 Copper, P = #390 Daffodil, Q = #791 Pistachio, R = #578 Rust, S = #190 Tundra, T = #880 Coffee, U = #292 Pine Forest, V = #1140 Granny Smith, W = #375 Flax, X = #524 Poppy, Y = #230 Yellow Ochre, Z = #587 Madder, and AA = #231 Bracken

A = #253 Seaweed, B = #140 Rye, C = #198 Peat, D = #180 Mist, E = #101 Shetland Black, F = #105 Eesit, G = #103 Sholmit, H = #125 Slate, I = #272 Fog, J = #183 Sand, K= #107 Mogit, L = #195 Moorland, M = #123 Oxford, N = #235 Grouse, O = #1270 Purple Haze, P = #106 Mooskit, Q = #238 Osprey, R = #108 Moorit, S = #175 Twilight, T = #102 Shaela, U = #1390 Highland Mist, V = #190 Tundra, W = #318 Woodgreen, X = #104 Natural White, Y = #122 Granite, Z = #237 Thistledown, and AA = #880 Coffee

BACK

With the smaller needles and G, cast on 130 (146, 162, 178, 194) stitches.

Begin the Rib Pattern, and work even until the piece measures approximately 3"/[7.5cm] from the beginning, ending after a wrong-side row.

Change to the larger needles, begin Row 1 of Man's Intarsia Pattern where indicated on the chart, and work even in the pattern until the piece measures approximately 16"/[40.5cm] from the beginning, ending after a wrong-side row.

Shape Armholes
Bind off 12 (12, 16, 20, 24) stitches at the beginning of the next 2 rows—106 (122, 130, 138, 146) stitches remain.

Continue even in the pattern until the piece measures approximately 24½ (25, 25½, 26, 26½)"/[62 (63.5, 65, 66, 67.5)cm] from the beginning, ending after a wrong-side row.

Shape Neck
NEXT ROW (RS): Work the pattern as established across the first 29 (37, 41, 45, 49) stitches, join a second ball of yarn, and bind off the center 48 stitches; work the pattern as established across to the end of the row.

Work both sides at once with separate balls of yarn and decrease 1 stitch at each neck edge once—28 (36, 40, 44, 48) stitches remain on each side.

Continue even in the pattern as established until the piece measures approximately 25 (25½, 26, 26½, 27)"/[63.5 (65, 66, 67.5, 68.5)cm] from the beginning, ending after a wrong-side row.

Shape Shoulders
Bind off 7 (9, 10, 11, 12) stitches at the beginning of the next 8 rows.

FRONT
Work the same as the Back until the piece measures approximately 23 (23½, 24, 24½, 25)"/[58.5 (59.5, 61, 62, 63.5)cm] from the beginning, ending after a wrong-side row.

Shape Neck

NEXT ROW (RS): Work the pattern as established across the first 43 (51, 55, 59, 63) stitches, join a second ball of yarn, and bind off the center 20 stitches; work the pattern as established to the end of the row.

Work both sides at once with separate balls of yarn. Bind off 6 stitches at each neck edge once, bind off 3 stitches at each neck edge once, bind off 2 stitches at each neck edge twice, then decrease 1 stitch at each neck edge twice—28 (36, 40, 44, 48) stitches remain each side.

Continue even until the piece measures the same as the back to the shoulders, ending after a wrong-side row.

Shape Shoulders

Work the same as for the Back.

SLEEVE (MAKE 2)

With the smaller needles and G, cast on 58 stitches.

Begin Rib Pattern, and work even until the piece measures approximately 3"/[7.5cm] from the beginning, ending after a wrong-side row.

Change to the larger needles, begin Row 1 of Man's Intarsia Pattern where indicated on chart, and increase 1 stitch each side every other row 0 (0, 3, 11, 21) times, every fourth row 11 (24, 28, 23, 16) times, then every sixth row 14 (4, 0, 0, 0) times, working new stitches into the pattern as they accumulate—108 (114, 120, 126, 132) stitches.

Continue even until the piece measures approximately 21½ (20½, 21, 20½, 20½)"/[54.5 (52, 53.5, 52, 52)cm] from the beginning.

Bind off.

FINISHING

Darn in all remaining yarn tails (page 135).

Block all pieces to the finished measurements (page 135).

Sew the left shoulder seam.

Neckband

With the right side facing, smaller needles, and G, pick up and knit 116 stitches evenly along the neckline.

Knit 3 rows.

Begin the Neckband Pattern, and work Rows 1–4 twice.

Change to G, and knit 4 rows.

Bind off.

Sew the right shoulder seam, including the side of the neckband.

Set in the sleeves.

Sew the sleeve and side seams.

scrap happy

The geometric motifs that begin with 4 stitches use approximately 7–7½ yd/[6.5–7m] of yarn, and the motif that begins with 12 stitches uses approximately 9¼ yd/[8.5m] of yarn, including tails.

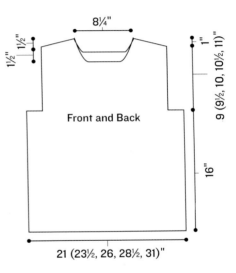

Front and Back

8¼"

1½" 1½"

9 (9½, 10, 10½, 11)"

1"

16"

21 (23½, 26, 28½, 31)"

Neckband Pattern

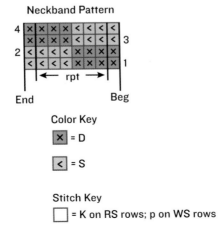

rpt

End   Beg

Color Key

⊠ = D

< = S

Stitch Key

□ = K on RS rows; p on WS rows

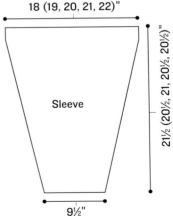

Sleeve

18 (19, 20, 21, 22)"

21½ (20½, 21, 20½, 20½)"

9½"

Intarsia Pattern, Rows 1–60

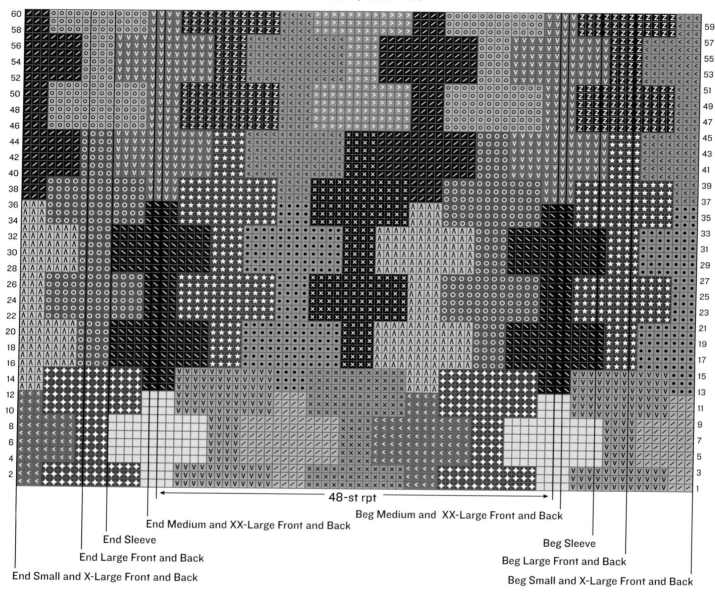

48-st rpt

End Medium and XX-Large Front and Back

End Sleeve

End Large Front and Back

End Small and X-Large Front and Back

Beg Medium and XX-Large Front and Back

Beg Sleeve

Beg Large Front and Back

Beg Small and X-Large Front and Back

Intarsia Pattern, Rows 61–120

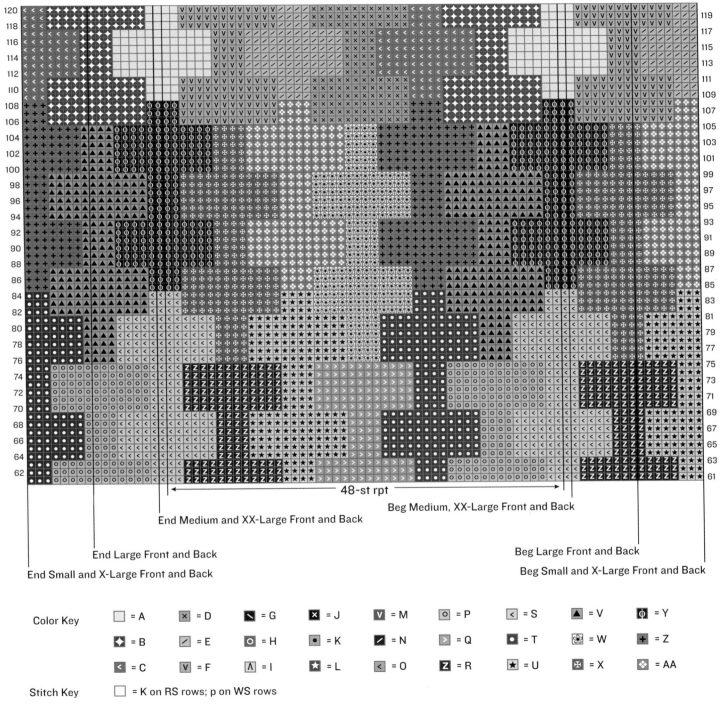

48-st rpt

Beg Medium, XX-Large Front and Back

End Medium and XX-Large Front and Back

End Large Front and Back

Beg Large Front and Back

End Small and X-Large Front and Back

Beg Small and X-Large Front and Back

Color Key

= A	⊠ = D	◣ = G	⊠ = J	V = M
⬖ = B	◢ = E	◉ = H	• = K	◤ = N
◂ = C	V = F	∧ = I	★ = L	◂ = O

◉ = P	◂ = S	▲ = V
▸ = Q	◙ = T	✳ = W
Z = R	★ = U	⊞ = X

φ = Y
+ = Z
◈ = AA

Stitch Key ☐ = K on RS rows; p on WS rows

the "worsted" case scenario

six projects using medium weight yarns

Too much worsted weight yarn languishing in your stash?

These six projects will put those leftovers to good use.

There's something for everyone here, from a vest for your

favorite guy (Strathaven, page 101) to a cuddly blanket

for Little One (Puzzle Play, page 79)—even a tote you

can make for yourself (Sausalito, page 83). Each pattern

uses medium weight yarn (CYCA category 4) or the

combinations of super fine, light, and fine yarns mentioned

in the chart on page 12.

puzzle play

Here's a showstopper that will make kids of all ages (and their parents) smile.

SKILL LEVEL
Intermediate

SIZE
One size

FINISHED MEASUREMENTS
Approximately 36" x 45¾"/[91.5 cm x 116cm]
(excluding the border)

MATERIALS
- Medium/worsted weight yarn (4)
  - 480 yd/[439m] of the main color (Q)
  - 120 yd/[110m] of each of 16 other colors A, B, C, D, E, F, G, H, I, J, K, L, M, N, O, and P)
- Size 7 [4.5 mm] circular knitting needle, 36"/[90cm] long, or size needed to obtain gauge
- 1 cable needle
- Bobbins (optional)
- Blunt-end yarn needle

The sample project uses Plymouth Yarn's Encore Worsted (4-medium/worsted weight; 75% acrylic/25% wool; each approximately 3½ oz/[100g] and 200 yd/ [183m]): #1382 Goldenrod (A), #235 Turquoise (B), #174 Claret (C), #457 Posy Pink (D), #1386 Barn Red (E), #1014 Gold (F), #1606 Violet (G), #4045 Skipper Blue (H), #3335 Lime (I), #1383 Orange (J), #137 Rose (K), #1317 Seaglass (L), #215 Butter Yellow (M), #1385 Cerise (N), #30 Turf Green (O), #1384 Regal Purple (P), and #133 Cornflower Blue (Q)

GAUGE
20 stitches and 28 rows = 4"/[10cm] in stockinette stitch.
To save time, take time to check gauge.

NOTES
- For the colorwork, use the intarsia technique (pages 129-130).
- A circular knitting needle is used in order to accommodate the large number of stitches; do not join at the end of rows.
- When increasing during the border, use the M1 knitwise and M1 purlwise techniques (page 131).

SPECIAL ABBREVIATION
2/2 LC: Slip 2 stitches to cn and hold in front; k2; k2 from cn.

STITCH PATTERNS
Puzzle Pattern (multiple of 60 stitches)
See the chart.

Alternative Colorway t

Alternative Colorway 2

Plymouth Yarn's *Encore Worsted*:
A = #670 Spruce Heather, B = #1232 Dusty Sage, C = #450 Light Kiwi, D = #9401 Fir Green, E = #801 Light Spruce, F = #3335 Spring Green, G = #54 Grass Green, H = #204 Bottle Green, I = #1405 Heathered Khaki Green, J = #451 Light Moss, K = #678 Heathered Mist Green, L = #668 Heather Forest, M = #1234 Darkest Hunter, N = #1233 Dark Moss, O = #1604 Pine, P = #1231 Lightest Sage, and Q = #217 Black

A = #1607 Berry, B = #1383 Orange, C = #1382 Sunshine, D = #175 Tobacco, E = #256 Crème, F = #386 Cherry Red, G = #453 Dark Salmon, H = #999 Chianti, I = #560 Heathered Burgundy, J = #1014 Goldenrod, K = #218 Aran, L = #456 Bronze, M = #9601 Lipstick Red, N = #215 Butter Yellow, O = #174 Claret, P = #1307 Light Salmon, and Q = #599 Chocolate

AFGHAN

With Q, cast on 180 stitches.

Cut Q, begin the Puzzle Pattern, and work even until the piece measures approximately 45¾"/[116cm] from the beginning, ending after Row 80 of the pattern.

Bind off with Q.

FINISHING

Border

With the right side facing and Q, pick up and knit 242 stitches along one long side of the afghan.

ROW 1 (WS): P2, *k2, p4, k2, p2; repeat from the * across.

ROW 2: K2, M1 knitwise, *p2, k4, p2, k2; repeat from the * across, ending the row with p2, k4, p2, M1 knitwise, k2.

ROW 3: P3, *k2, p4, k2, p2; repeat from the * across, ending the row with k2, p4, k2, p3.

ROW 4: K2, M1 knitwise, k1, *p2, 2/2 LC, p2, k2; repeat from the * across, ending the row with p2, 2/2 LC, k1, M1 knitwise, k2.

ROW 5: P4, *k2, p4, k2, p2; repeat from the * across, ending the row with k2, p4, k2, p4.

ROW 6: K2, M1 purlwise, k2, *p2, k4, p2, k2; repeat from the * across, ending the row with, M1 purlwise, k2.

ROW 7: P2, k1, p2, *k2, p4, k2, p2; repeat from the * across, ending the row with k1, p2.

ROW 8: K2, M1 purlwise, p1, *k2, p2, 2/2 LC, p2; repeat from the * across, ending the row with, k2, p1, M1 purlwise, k2.

ROW 9: P2, k2, *p2, k2, p4, k2; repeat from the * across, ending the row with p2, k2, p2.

ROW 10: K2, M1 knitwise, *p2, k2, p2, k4; repeat from the* across, ending the row with p2, k2, p2, M1 knitwise, k2.

ROW 11: P3, *k2, p2, k2, p4; repeat from the * across, ending the row with k2, p2, k2, p3.

ROW 12: K2, M1 knitwise, k1, *p2, k2, p2, 2/2 LC; repeat from the * across, ending the row with p2, k2, p2, k1, M1 knitwise, k2.

ROW 13: P4, *k2, p2, k2, p4; repeat from the * across.

ROW 14: K2, M1 knitwise, k2, *p2, k2, p2, k4; repeat from the * across, ending the row with p2, k2, p2, k2, M1 knitwise, k2.

ROW 15: P5, *k2, p2, k2, p4; repeat from the * across, ending the row with p1.

ROW 16: K2, M1 knitwise, k3, *p2, k2, p2, 2/2 LC; repeat from the * across, ending the row with p2, k2, p2, k3, M1 knitwise, k2.

ROW 17: P6, *k2, p2, k2, p4; repeat from the * across, ending the row with p2.

ROW 18: K2, M1 purlwise, k4, *p2, k2, p2, k4; repeat from the * across, ending the row with M1 purlwise, k2.

ROW 19: P2, k1, p4, *k2, p2, k2, p4; repeat from the * across, ending the row with k1, p2.

ROW 20: K2, M1 purlwise, p1, *2/2 LC, p2, k2, p2; repeat from the * across, ending the row with 2/2 LC, p1, M1 purlwise, k2.

ROW 21: P2, k2, *p4, k2, p2, k2; repeat from the * across, ending the row with p4, k2, p2.

Bind off *loosely* in pattern.

Repeat for the other long side.

With the right side facing, pick up and knit 182 stitches along one short side of the afghan.

Work the border the same as for the long sides.

Bind off *loosely* in pattern.

Repeat for the other short side.

Using the mattress stitch (pages 135–136), sew the corners together.

Darn in all remaining yarn tails (page 135).

Block the piece to the finished measurements (page 135).

scrap happy

Each individual section of color requires 8 yd/[7.5m] of yarn, including tails. Precut your yarn to that length to keep the knitting and finishing as easy as possible.

Puzzle Pattern

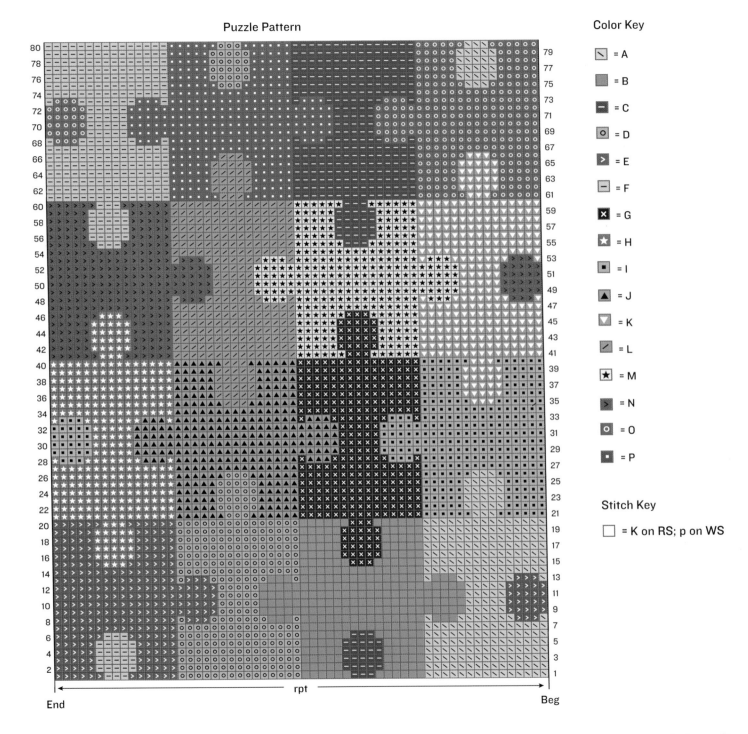

sausalito

Use up yarn in your stash while knitting this practical bag. The textured pattern is fun to knit and will accommodate as many colors as you'd like.

SKILL LEVEL
Intermediate

SIZE
One size

FINISHED MEASUREMENTS
16" x 14" x 4"/[40.5cm x 35.5cm x 10cm]
(*excluding straps*)

MATERIALS
- Medium/worsted weight yarn (4)
  - 1,000 yd/[914.5m] in the main color (A)
  - 26 yd/[24m] in each of 7 contrasting colors (B, C, D, E, F, G, and H)
  - 13 yd/[12m] in each of 5 other contrast colors (I, J, K, L, and M)
- Size 8 [5mm] circular knitting needle, 24"/[60cm] long, or size needed to obtain gauge
- Size 6 [4mm] knitting needles, or size needed to obtain gauge
- Blunt-end yarn needle
- ¾ yd/[.5m] fabric for lining
- ¾ yd/[.5m] iron-on interface for added stability (optional)
- Matching sewing thread
- Sharp sewing needle
- Stitch holder
- Pins

The sample project uses Cascade Yarn's 220 Superwash (*4-medium/worsted weight; 100% wool; each approximately 3½ oz/[100g] and 220 yd/[200m]*): #805 Bright Magenta (A), #807 Lipstick Pink (B), #848 Skipper Blue (C), #907 Tangerine (D), #851 Spring Green (E), #806 Blue Pink (F), #813 Cadet Blue (G), #827 Ripe Peach (H), #906 Meadow Green (I), #880 Merlot (J), #884 Baby Boy Blue (K), #825 Gold (L), and #887 Pea Green (M)

GAUGE
23 stitches and 26 rows = 4"/[10cm] in the Twisted Rib Pattern with the smaller needles.
22 stitches and 20 rows = 4"/[10cm] in the Star Pattern with the larger needle.
To save time, take time to check gauge.

NOTE
- The circular needle is used in order to accommodate the large number of stitches. Do not join at the end of rounds; instead, work back and forth in rows.

SPECIAL ABBREVIATION
Star: P3tog, leaving the stitches on the left-hand needle, yarn over, then purl the 3 stitches together again, slipping them off the needle together.

STITCH PATTERNS
Twisted Rib Pattern (multiple of 2 + 1 stitches)
ROW 1 (RS): K1-tbl, *p1-tbl, k1-tbl; repeat from the * across.
ROW 2: P1-tbl, *k1-tbl, p1-tbl; repeat from the * across.
Repeat Rows 1 and 2 for the pattern.

Star Pattern (multiple of 4 + 2 stitches)
ROW 1 (RS): With A, p1, *k1, p1; repeat from the * to the last stitch, ending the row with p1.
ROW 2: With A, k2, *star, k1; repeat from the * across.
ROW 3: With a contrasting color, repeat Row 1.
ROW 4: With the same contrasting color used in the last row, k2, p1, k1, *star, k1; repeat from the * to the last 2 stitches, ending the row with p1, k1.
Repeat Rows 1–4 for the pattern.

K1 P1 Rib Pattern (multiple of 2 stitches)
PATTERN ROW (RS): *K1, p1; repeat from the * across.

Stripe Pattern
Work *2 rows with the main color (A), 2 rows with a contrast color; repeat from the * for the pattern.

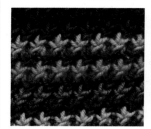

Alternative Colorway 1

Alternative Colorway 2

Cascade Yarn's *220 Superwash*: A = #863 Chocolate, B = #841 Sage, C = #858 Toffee, D = #853 Maize, E = #888 Olive, F = #822 Orange, G = #876 Butterscotch, H = #866 Bottle Green, I = #823 Persimmon, J = #828 Dark Camel, K = #801 Forest, L = #855 Claret, and M = #880 Burgundy

A = #831 Rosy Pink, B = #903 Hot Pink, C = #834 Hibiscus, D = #884 Baby Boy Blue, E = #826 Mango, F = #827 Papaya, G = #820 Lemon, H = #814 Periwinkle, I = #821 Sunshine, J = #877 Goldenrod, K = #901 Posy Pink, and L = #835 Petal Pink

BASE OF TOTE
With the circular needle and A, cast on 23 stitches.

Begin the Twisted Rib Pattern and work even until the piece measures approximately 16"/[40.5 cm] from the beginning, ending after a wrong-side row. Do not fasten off.

Begin Body of Tote
With the right side facing, the circular needle, and A, working along the base piece of tote, pick up and knit 2 stitches in the upper right corner, 21 stitches along the first short edge, 88 stitches along the first long edge, 22 stitches along the second short edge, 87 stitches along the second long edge, and 2 stitches in the upper right corner—222 stitches total.

Continue in the Stripe Pattern, and beginning with Row 2, work the Star Pattern back and forth in rows until the piece measures approximately 14"/[35.5cm] from the base, ending after a wrong-side row worked in one of the contrast colors. Do not bind off.

Upper Trim
Change to the smaller needles, begin the K1 P1 Rib Pattern, and work even for 8 rows.

Bind off in pattern.

FINISHING
Darn in all remaining yarn tails (page 135).

Block the piece to the finished measurements (page 135).

Lining
Cut the lining to fit the bag.

[Optional: Cut the iron-on interface to fit the lining. Follow the manufacturer's instructions to apply to the wrong side of the lining fabric.]

Using mattress stitch (pages 135–136), sew the side seam of the bag.

Sew the lining into place, folding ¾"/[1cm] hems to the wrong side.

Fold the upper trim to the wrong side and loosely sew into place.

Straps
With the smaller needles and A, cast on 17 stitches.

Begin the Twisted Rib Pattern, and work even until the piece measures approximately 114"/[289.5cm] from the beginning, ending after a wrong-side row.

Slip the stitches onto a holder.

Use mattress stitch to join the cast-on and bind-off ends of the strap together, being careful not to twist the strap.

Pin the strap to the bag following the diagram or as follows:

With the strap seam centered at the base of the bag 3"/[7.5cm] from the left edge, pin the strap to the bag until it reaches the front and back top edges; position the upper loop of the strap 3"/[7.5cm] from the right edge of the base and pin this side of the strap to the bag until it reaches the front and back top edges, making sure that both handles (the 2 unsewn loops) are the same length.

With coordinating sewing thread and sharp needle, sew the strap into place.

Reinforce the strap (page 37).

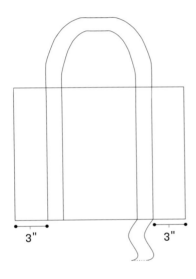

DIY *easy to handle*

The sample tote in the photograph has long shoulder straps. For a hand-held tote, simply make the strap shorter! It's as easy as that!

cables and colors

Believe it or not, your leftover yarn can become the main feature of a beautiful sweater. Select a main color to tie all the others together, and just knit away.

SKILL LEVEL
Intermediate

SIZES
Small (Medium, Large, 1X, 2X, 3X). Instructions are for the smallest size, with changes for other sizes noted in parentheses as necessary.

FINISHED MEASUREMENTS
Bust: 34 (38, 42, 46, 50, 54)"/[86.5 (96.5, 106.5, 117, 127, 137)cm]
Length: 24 (24³/₄, 25¹/₂, 25³/₄, 26¹/₄, 26³/₄)"/[61 (63, 65, 65.5, 67, 68)cm]

MATERIALS
- Medium/worsted weight yarn (4)
  - 1,050 (1,200, 1,300, 1,450, 1,550, 1,700) yd/[960 (1,097, 1,189, 1,326, 1,417, 1,554)m] in the main color (A)
  - 27 (30, 32, 36, 38, 41) yd/[25 (27.5, 29, 33, 35, 37.5)m] in B
  - 42 (56, 67, 85, 99, 119) yd/[38.5 (51, 61, 78, 90.5, 109)m] in C
  - 11 (12, 13, 14, 15, 16) yd/[10 (11, 12, 13, 14, 14.5)m] in D
  - 25 (29, 30, 34, 36, 39) yd/[23 (26.5, 27.5, 31, 33, 36)m] in E
  - 32 (37, 38, 43, 45, 49) yd/[29 (34, 35, 39, 41, 45)m] in F
  - 20 (25, 27, 30, 34, 39) yd/[18 (23, 24, 27.5, 31, 36)m] in G
  - 18 (21, 21, 24, 25, 27) yd/[16.5 (19, 19, 22, 23, 25)m] in H
  - 32 (37, 38, 43, 45, 49) yd/[29 (34, 35, 39.5, 41, 45)m] in I
  - 17 (20, 21, 23, 24, 27) yd/[15.5 (18, 19, 21, 22, 25)m] in J
  - 18 (21, 21, 24, 25, 27) yd/[16.5 (19, 19, 22, 23, 25)m] in K
  - 7 (8, 9, 10, 11, 12) yd/[6.5 (7.5, 8, 9, 10, 11)m] in L
  - 29 (33, 40, 49, 53, 58) yd/[26.5 (30, 36.5, 45, 48.5, 53)m] in M
  - 15 (17, 21, 27, 29, 31) yd/[14 (15.5, 19, 25, 26.5, 28.5)m] in N
- Size 7 [4.5mm] circular knitting needle, 32"/[80cm] long (or longer for larger sizes), or size needed to obtain gauge
- Size 7 [4.5mm] circular knitting needle, 40"/[100cm] long (or longer for larger sizes), or size needed to obtain gauge
- Size 6 [4mm] double-pointed knitting needles (set of 4)
- Size 7 [4.5mm] double-pointed knitting needles (set of 4), or size needed to obtain gauge
- Size 7 [4.5mm] circular knitting needle, 24"/[60cm] long (or longer for larger sizes), or size needed to obtain gauge
- Size 7 [4.5mm] circular knitting needle, 16"/[40cm] long, or size needed to obtain gauge
- Size 6 [4mm] circular knitting needle, 16"/[40cm] long
- 1 stitch marker
- 1 cable needle
- 2 stitch holders (optional)
- Blunt-end yarn needle

The sample project uses Brown Sheep Company's Nature Spun Worsted (4-medium/worsted weight; 100% wool; each approximately 3¹/₂ oz/[100g] and 245 yd/[224m]): #124 Butterscotch (A), #111 Plumberry (B), #105 Bougainvillea (C), #104 Grecian Olive (D), #N17 French Clay (E), #N89 Roasted Coffee (F), #146

Pomegranate (G), #144 Limestone (H), #136 Chocolate Kisses (I), #308 Sunburst Gold (J), #156 Irish Shamrock (K), #225 Brick Road (L), #522 Nervous Green (M), and #209 Wood Moss (N)

GAUGE

24 stitches and 28 rounds = 4"/[10cm] in the Cable Pattern with the larger circular needle.

22 stitches and 28 rounds = 4"/[10cm] in Yoke Patterns 1, 2, and 3 with the larger circular needle.

To save time, take time to check gauge.

NOTES

- The body and sleeves of this garment are made in the round from the bottom up; at the underarm, the body and sleeves are joined together, and the colorful yoke is worked in the round.
- For the yoke, start with the longest circular needle and change to shorter ones when necessary to accommodate the number of stitches.
- For the sleeves, begin with double-pointed needles and change to a circular needle when there are enough stitches accumulated to do so.
- Use stranded technique (pages 133–134) for the colorwork. If 3 colors are used within a round, be sure to carry them loosely across the fabric the same way 2 colors would be worked.
- Each size will work the Yoke Charts with different numbers of rounds as follows:

  Small: Work the 3 charts as presented.

  Medium: Work extra rounds as follows: Chart 1: work [Round 2] 3 times; Chart 2: work [Round 1] twice; Chart 3: work [Round 12] twice.

  Large: Work extra rounds as follows: Chart 1: work [Round 2] 5 times; Chart 2: work [Rounds 1 and 5] twice; Chart 3: work [Rounds 6 and 14] twice.

  1X: Work extra rounds as follows: Chart 1: work [Round 2] 7 times; Chart 2: work [Rounds 1, 5, and 10] twice; Chart 3: work [Rounds 6, 8, and 14] twice.

  2X: Work extra rounds as follows: Chart 1: work [Round 2] 9 times; Chart 2: work [Rounds 1, 5, 10, and

  14] twice; Chart 3: work [Rounds 6 and 8] twice and [Round 14] 3 times.

  3X: Work extra rounds as follows: Chart 1: work [Round 2] 11 times; Chart 2: work [Round 1] 3 times and [Rounds 5, 10, and 14] twice; Chart 3: work [Rounds 6 and 8] twice and [Round 14] 4 times.

SPECIAL ABBREVIATIONS

RT (Right Twist): Slip 1 stitch to cn and hold in back, k1, k1 from cn.

2/2 LC: Slip 2 stitches to cn and hold in front, k2, k2 from cn.

2/2 RC: Slip 2 stitches to cn and hold in back, k2, k2 from cn.

STITCH PATTERNS

Rib Pattern (multiple of 12 stitches)

ROUND 1: *P1, RT, p2, k2, p2, k2, p1; repeat from the * around.

ROUND 2: *P1, k2 [p2, k2] twice, p1; repeat from the * around.

Repeat Rounds 1 and 2 for the pattern.

Or see the chart.

Cable Pattern (multiple of 12 stitches)

ROUND 1: *P1, RT, p2, k2, 2/2 LC, p1; repeat from the * around.

ROUND 2: *P1, k2, p2, k6, p1; repeat from the * around.

ROUND 3: *P1, RT, p2, 2/2 RC, k2, p1; repeat from the * around.

ROUND 4: As for Round 2.

Repeat Rounds 1–4 for the pattern.

Or see the chart.

Yoke Pattern 1 (multiple of 6 stitches)

See the chart.

Yoke Pattern 2 (multiple of 4 stitches)

See the chart.

Yoke Pattern 3 (multiple of 4 stitches)

See the chart.

Neckband Pattern (multiple of 4 stitches)

ROUND 1: *P1, RT, p1; repeat from the * around.

ROUND 2: *P1, k2, p1; repeat from the * around.

Repeat Rounds 1 and 2 for the pattern.

Or see the chart.

Alternative Colorway 1

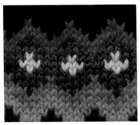

Alternative Colorway 2

Brown Sheep Company's *Nature Spun Worsted*: A = #N39 Navy Nite, B = #207 Alpine Violet, C = #116 Blue Boy, D = #109 Spring Green, E = #120 Cresting Wave, F = #N24 Evergreen, G = #N85 Peruvian Pink, H = #205 Regal Purple, I = #103 Deep Sea, J = #N60 Purple Splendor, K = #144 Limestone, L = #N62 Amethyst, M = #112 Elf Green, and N = #N78 Turquoise Wonder

A = #601 Pepper, B = #145 Salmon, C = #108 Cherry Delight, D = #305 Impasse Yellow, E = #207 Alpine Violet, F = #N54 Orange You Glad, G = #205 Regal Purple, H = #N85 Peruvian Pink, I = #N65 Sapphire, J = #N87 Victorian Pink, K = #105 Bougainvillea, L = #N62 Amethyst, M = #N42 Royal Purple, and N = #N60 Purple Splendor

BODY

With one of the larger circular needles and A, cast on 204 (228, 252, 276, 300, 324) stitches.

Place a marker for the beginning of the round, and join, being careful not to twist the stitches on the needle.

Begin the Rib Pattern and work even until the piece measures approximately 1½"/[4cm] from the beginning, ending after Round 2 of the pattern.

Begin the Cable Pattern and work even until the piece measures approximately 16¼"/[41.5cm] from the beginning, ending after an even-numbered round.

Divide for Underarm

Bind off 20 (22, 26, 28, 30, 32) stitches for the underarm, knit across the next 82 (92, 100, 110, 120, 130) stitches, and slip them onto a holder or a length of scrap yarn for the front, bind off the next 20 (22, 26, 28, 30, 32) stitches for the underarm, knit across the next 82 (92, 100, 110, 120, 130) stitches and slip them onto a holder or a length of scrap yarn for the back.

SLEEVE (MAKE 2)

With the smaller double-pointed needles and A, cast on 60 stitches.

Divide evenly onto 3 needles. Place a marker and join, being careful not to twist the stitches on the needles.

Begin the Rib Pattern and work even until the piece measures approximately 1½"/[4cm] from the beginning.

Change to the larger double-pointed needles, begin the Cable Pattern, and work 1 round of the pattern.

INCREASE ROUND: P1, M1 knitwise (page 131), work the established Cable Pattern to the last stitch, M1 knitwise, p1—62 stitches.

Continue the pattern and repeat the Increase Round every fourth round 0 (0, 0, 0, 0, 8) times, every sixth round 0 (0, 0, 11, 9, 15) times, every eighth round 0 (3, 2, 6, 8, 0) times, every tenth round 0 (8, 9, 0, 0, 0) times, every sixteenth round 1 (0, 0,

0, 0, 0) time, then every eighteenth round 4 (0, 0, 0, 0, 0) times, working new stitches into the Cable Pattern as they accumulate—72 (84, 84, 96, 96, 108) stitches.

Continue even until the piece measures approximately 17 (18, 18½, 19½, 19¾, 20)"/[43 (45.5, 47, 49.5, 50, 51)cm] from the beginning, ending the last round 10 (11, 13, 14, 15, 16) stitches before the end of the round.

Bind off the next 20 (22, 26, 28, 30, 32) stitches for the underarm. Slip the remaining 52 (62, 58, 68, 66, 76) stitches onto a holder or piece of scrap yarn.

Repeat for the second sleeve, but leave the stitches on the needle.

YOKE
With the right sides facing, slip the stitches from the Back, one Sleeve, the Front, and the other Sleeve onto the longest larger circular needle—268 (308, 316, 356, 372, 412) stitches.

Place a marker between the back and the right sleeve stitches, and join.

scrap happy

When choosing the scrap yarn for the colorful yoke on this sweater, remember that colors used earlier in the yoke will require more yardage; save the ones you have less of for later on in the yoke.

With A, knit one round, using the k2tog technique to decrease 46 (50, 52, 56, 60, 70) stitches evenly around—222 (258, 264, 300, 312, 342) stitches remain.

Begin Yoke Pattern 1, working the appropriate number of rounds (see Notes).

NEXT ROUND: With A, knit around, using the k2tog technique to decrease 70 (86, 76, 92, 88, 98) stitches evenly around—152 (172, 188, 208, 224, 244) stitches remain.

Begin Yoke Pattern 2, working the appropriate number of rounds (see Notes).

NEXT ROUND: With M, knit around, using the k2tog technique to decrease 52 (60, 64, 68, 76, 84)

stitches evenly around—100 (112, 124, 140, 148, 160) stitches remain.

Begin Yoke Pattern 3, working the appropriate number of rounds (see Notes).

NEXT ROUND: With A, knit around, using the k2tog technique to decrease 12 (20, 28, 36, 40, 48) stitches evenly around—88 (92, 96, 104, 108, 112) stitches remain.

FINISHING
With the smaller circular needle and A, begin Neckband Pattern, and work even until the neckband measures approximately 3½"/ [9cm] from the beginning.

Bind off *loosely* in the pattern.

Use mattress stitch (pages 135–136) to sew the underarm seams.

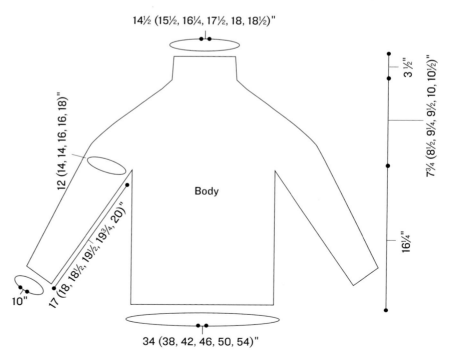

14½ (15½, 16¼, 17½, 18, 18½)"

12 (14, 14, 16, 16, 18)"

3 ½"

7¾ (8½, 9¼, 9½, 10, 10½)"

Body

16¼"

17 (18, 18½, 19½, 19¾, 20)"

10"

34 (38, 42, 46, 50, 54)"

Cable Pattern

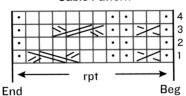

End Beg

Rib Pattern

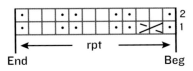

End Beg

Yoke Pattern 1

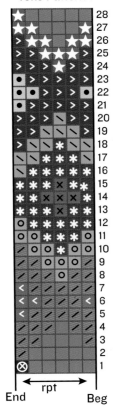

End Beg

Neckband Pattern

End Beg

Yoke Pattern 2

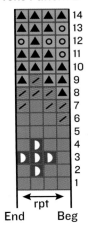

End Beg

Yoke Pattern 3

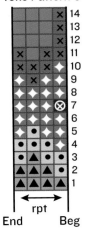

End Beg

Color Key

= A = E = I = M

= B = F = J = N

= C = G = K

= D = H = L

Stitch Key

□ = K

• = P

= Right Twist = Slip next st onto cn and hold in back; k1; k1 from cn **or** k2tog, leaving them on LH needle; insert point of RH needle between these 2 sts and k the first st again

= Slip 2 sts onto cn and hold in back; k2; k2 from cn

= Slip 2 sts onto cn and hold in front; k2; k2 from cn

⊗ = Bobble = Knit into (front, back, front) of next st, turn; p1, (p1, yarn over, p1) all into next st, p1, turn; k5, turn; p2tog, p1, p2tog, turn; slip 2 sts at once knitwise, k1, p2sso

roundabout

Wear this eye-popping jacket and you'll be the center of attention both coming and going! Its circular construction is fun to knit and makes great use of your stash.

SKILL LEVEL
Intermediate

SIZES
Small (Medium, Large, 1X, 2X, 3X). Instructions are for the smallest size, with changes for other sizes noted in parentheses as necessary.

FINISHED MEASUREMENTS
Bust (*closed*): 35 (39, 43, 47, 51, 55)"/[89 (99, 109, 119.5, 129.5, 139.5)cm]
Length (*when the jacket is worn the short way*): 17 1/2 (19 1/2, 21 1/2, 23 1/2, 25 1/2, 27 1/2)"/[44.5 (49.5, 54.5, 59.5, 65, 70)cm]
Length (*when the jacket is worn the long way*): 23 3/4 (26 1/2, 29, 31 3/4, 34 1/2, 37)"/[60.5 (67.5, 73.5, 80.5, 87.5, 94)cm]

MATERIALS
- Medium/worsted weight yarn (4)
  – 1,300 (1,550, 1,825, 2,150, 2,475, 2,825) yd/[1,188.5 (1,417.5, 1,669, 1,966, 2,263, 2,583)m] in assorted textures and colors
- Size 8 [5mm] double-pointed knitting needles (set of 5), or size needed to obtain gauge
- Size 8 [5mm] circular knitting needle, 16"/[40cm] long, or size needed to obtain gauge
- Size 8 [5mm] circular knitting needle, 24"/[60cm] long, or size needed to obtain gauge
- Size 8 [5mm] circular knitting needle, 32"/[80cm] long or size needed to obtain gauge
- Size 9 [5.5 mm] circular knitting needle, 32"/[80cm] long
- Size 10 [6mm] circular knitting needle, 32"/[80cm] long
- Size 10 [6.5mm] circular knitting needle, 32"/[80cm] long
- Size I/9 [5.5mm] crochet hook (for provisional cast on)
- 8 Stitch markers, one in a contrast color to mark the beginning of rounds
- Blunt-end yarn needle

The sample project uses a magic ball created with overhand knots (page 21) until the armholes, then Russian join (page 22) for the rest of the garment, using a variety of yarns from Classic Elite as follows:
- Giselle (*4-medium/worsted weight; 64% kid mohair/25% wool/11% nylon; each approximately 1 3/4 oz/[50g] and 225 yd/[205.5m]*) in #4179 Harem Purple, #4105 Moorish Nights, #4156 Navarra, #4120 Darrow River, #4109 Moroccan Teal, and #4104 Myrtle
- Lush (*4-medium/worsted weight; 50% angora/50% wool; each approximately 1 3/4 oz [50g] and 123 yd/ [112.5m]*) in #4407 Thistle, #4457 Blueberry, #4430 Sky Blue, #4479 Patrician Purple, #4467 Vintage Blue, #4420 Aqua Foam, and #4446 Spruce

- Portland Tweed *(4-medium/worsted weight; 50% virgin wool/25% alpaca/25% viscose; each approximately 1¾ oz/[50g] and 120 yd/[109.5m])* in *#5020 Glacier, #5057 Hudson Bay, #5047 Misty Blue, #5095 Amaranth, #5077 Folkestone, #5046 Best Teal,* and *#5004 Tidal Foam*
- Waterlily *(4-medium/worsted weight; 100% extra fine merino; each approximately 1¾ oz/[50g] and 90 yd/[82.5m])* in *#1957 Wedgewood, #1924 Blueberry, #1947 Lake,* and *#1915 Eucalyptus*
- Kumara *(4-medium/worsted weight; 85% extra fine merino/15% baby camel; each approximately 1¾ oz/[50g] and 128 yd/[117m])* in *#5704 Lombardy Blue* and *#5757 Blueprint*
- La Gran *(4-medium/worsted weight; 78.4% mohair/17.3% wool/4.3% nylon; each approximately 1¾ oz/[50g] and 108 yd/[99m])* in *#6542 Lavender Ice, #61520 Blue Topaz, #6554 French Lilac,* and *#6562 Blue Spruce*
- Solstice *(4-medium/worsted weight; 70% organic cotton/30% merino wool; each approximately 1¾ oz/[50g] and 100 yd/[91.5m])* in *#2354 Lavender Mist, #2342 Blue Moon,* and *#2349 Calais*

GAUGE

18 stitches and 24 rounds = 4"/[10cm] in the pattern with the smallest-size needles.

To save time, take time to check gauge.

NOTES

- This garment is a circle that starts at the center back and grows larger until the back width measurement is reached; then, two slits are formed for the armholes, with stitches placed onto scrap yarn to be picked up later for sleeves; once the body is completed, the sleeves are worked downward to the lower edge.
- For the body, start with double-pointed needles and change to circular needles when enough stitches accumulate to do so.
- For the sleeves, start with a circular needle, and change to double-pointed needles when necessary; the smaller sizes might require double-pointed needles for the entire length of the sleeves.

SPECIAL ABBREVIATIONS

K1f&b = Knit into the front and back of next stitch (page 130).

Alternative Colorway 1

Classic Elite's *Giselle* in #4101 Cloud; *Lush* in #4416 Natural; *Kumara* in #5716 Crema; *La Gran* in #6516 Natural, #6501 Bleached White, and #6503 Light Grey; *Solstice* in #2301 White and #2316 Natural

Alternative Colorway 2

Giselle in #4132 Madrid Red; *Lush* in #4458 Lipstick, #4455 Crabapple, and #4442 Cute Pink; *Waterlily* in #1953 Strawberry and #1919 Petunia; *Kumara* in #5758 Mars Red; *La Gran* in #6527 Chinese Red, #6541 Cape Cranberry, #61555 Tangerine, and #6572 Underappreciated Green; *Solstice* in #2358 Geranium, #2385 Orange Peel, #2389 Pink Tulip, and #2335 Pampas

BODY

With your magic ball of yarn, cast on 8 stitches onto one double-pointed needle.

Divide the stitches between 4 double-pointed needles. Join, being careful not to twist stitches on the needles. Place the contrasting-colored marker for beginning of the rounds.

ROUND 1 (RS): [K1f&b in next stitch, place a marker] 7 times, k1f&b in next stitch—16 stitches.

ROUND 2 AND ALL EVEN-NUMBERED ROUNDS: Knit around.

INCREASE ROUND: *Knit to 1 stitch before the marker, k1f&b, slip the marker; repeat from the * around—8 stitches increased.

Continue in this way, increasing 1 stitch before each marker every other round until there are 28 (31, 34, 37, 40, 43) stitches between markers, ending after an increase round—224 (248, 272, 296, 320, 344) stitches.

Make Slits for Sleeves

NEXT ROUND: K28 (31, 34, 37, 40, 43); *slip the next 28 (31, 34, 37, 40, 43) stitches onto a piece of scrap yarn; with the working yarn, use a provisional cast on (page 000) to cast on 28 (31, 34, 37, 40, 43) stitches for one sleeve opening (replacing the stitches on hold)**; k56 (62, 68, 74, 80, 86); repeat from the * to the ** for the second sleeve opening; k84 (93, 102, 111, 120, 129) to end the round.

Begin using the Russian join (page 22) to make the magic ball, and continue as before, increasing 1 stitch between the markers every other round until there are 55 (62, 69, 78, 83, 89) stitches between markers, ending after a plain, even-numbered round—440 (496, 552, 624, 664, 712) stitches.

Border

NEXT ROUND: *K2tog, k1, yarn over, k2, yarn over, k1, ssk; repeat from the * around.

NEXT ROUND: P3, *k2, p6; repeat from the * to the last 5 stitches, ending the round with k2, p3.

Repeat the last 2 rounds twice more.

Change to the size 9 circular needle, and repeat the last 2 rounds once more.

Change to the size 10 circular needle, and repeat the last 2 rounds once more.

Change to the size 11 circular needle, and repeat the last 2 rounds once more.

NEXT ROUND: Bind off *loosely* in pattern.

SLEEVE (MAKE 2)

Remove 28 (31, 34, 37, 40, 43) stitches from one provisional cast-on and place the live stitches on the 16"/[40cm] circular needle (for smaller sizes, see Notes); slip the stitches that are on hold for the same sleeve onto the same circular needle—56 (62, 68, 74, 80, 86) stitches.

Place a marker at the underarm for the beginning of rounds, join your magic ball of yarn and knit even until the sleeve measures approximately 1"/[2.5cm].

For the Size Small Sleeve *Only*
Continue even until the sleeve measures approximately 12"/[30.5cm].

For All Sizes *Except* **Small**
(*Instructions are for the smallest size, with changes for other sizes noted in parentheses as necessary. When a size is not being worked, there is a blank space inserted as a place holder.*)

NEXT ROUND (DECREASE ROUND): *Ssk, knit around until 2 stitches remain in the round, ending the round with k2tog—__ (60, 66, 72, 78, 84) stitches.

Repeat the Decrease Round every __ (22nd, 11th, 13th, 8th, 6th) round __ (2, 5, 4, 7, 10) times—__ (56, 56, 64, 64, 64) stitches remain.

Continue even until the sleeve measures approximately 12"/[30.5cm].

For All Sizes
Work 12 rows of the Border on 56 (56, 56, 64, 64, 64) stitches same as for the body.

Bind off in pattern.

Repeat for second sleeve.

scrap happy

Create a magic ball of different textures and colors to ensure a knockout, one-of-a-kind garment. Be sure to use varying lengths from 12"/[30.5cm] to 36"/[91.5cm] of each yarn, selecting yarns randomly. Use simple overhand knots until you reach the slits for the sleeves, but then change to the Russian join (page 22) so the yarn tails don't appear on the collar once it is folded to the right side.

DIY — *a vested interest*

If you'd rather knit a sleeveless version of this design, omit the sleeves and work a simple edging around the arm slits like this: Remove 28 (31, 34, 37, 40, 43) stitches from one provisional cast-on and place on 16"/[40cm] circular needle (for smaller sizes, see Notes), then slip the stitches from the same sleeve onto the same circular needle—56 (62, 68, 74, 80, 86) stitches. Place a marker at the underarm for the beginning of the round, and join your magic ball of yarn. Knit the first round, decreasing 7 (7, 8, 8, 9, 9) stitches evenly around—49 (55, 60, 66, 71, 77) stitches remain. Alternately purl one round and knit one round for 1"/[2.5cm]. Bind off loosely.

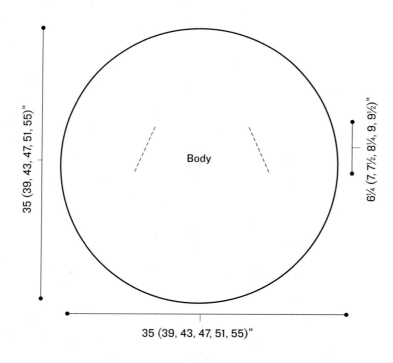

35 (39, 43, 47, 51, 55)"

6¼ (7, 7½, 8¼, 9, 9½)"

Body

35 (39, 43, 47, 51, 55)"

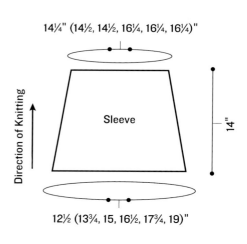

14¼" (14½, 14½, 16¼, 16¼, 16¼)"

Direction of Knitting

Sleeve

14"

12½ (13¾, 15, 16½, 17¾, 19)"

tamara's
wrap

tamara's wrap

Linen stitch creates an amazing fabric: It can accommodate lots of seemingly unrelated colors and blend them into a cohesive colorway. This project uses tints and shades of analogous colors (reds, orange, pinks, and lavender). The yarn tails are incorporated into the fringe, making finishing easy!

SKILL LEVEL
Advanced Beginner

SIZE
One size

FINISHED MEASUREMENTS
Width: 25"/[63.5cm]
Length: 64"/[162.5cm] (*excluding fringe*)

MATERIALS
- Medium/worsted weight yarn
  - 133 yd/[122m] in each of 11 colors (A, B, C, D, E, F, G, H, I, J, and K)
- Size 10½ [6.5 mm] circular knitting needle, 36"/[90cm] long, or size needed to obtain gauge
- Blunt-end yarn needle

The sample project uses Nashua Yarn's Creative Focus Worsted (4-medium/worsted weight; 75% wool/25% alpaca; each approximately 3½ oz/[100g] and 220 yd/[200m]): #2055 Carmine (A), #1837 Soft Pink (B), #2190 Copper (C), #4053 Lavender (D), #1890 Magenta (E), #1636 Salmon (F), #0712 Lavender Heather (G), #2120 Brick (H), #2755 Deep Rose (I), #2095 Cayenne (J), and #0066 Carnation (K)

GAUGE
18 stitches and 35 rows = 4"/[10cm] in linen stitch.
To save time, take time to check gauge.

NOTES
- For ease in finishing, begin and end every row with a 6"/[15cm] tail. These yarn tails will later be incorporated into the fringe.
- Always slip stitches purlwise (page 132).

STITCH PATTERNS
Linen Stitch (multiple of 2 + 1 stitches)
ROW 1 (RS): *K1, slip the next stitch with the yarn in front; repeat from the * across, ending the row with k1.
ROW 2: K1, *p1, slip the next stitch with the yarn in back; repeat from the * across, ending the row with p1, k1.
Repeat Rows 1 and 2 for the pattern.

Stripe Pattern
Work 1 row *each* with *B, C, D, E, F, G, H, I, J, K, A; repeat from the * for the pattern.

Alternative Colorway 1

Alternative Colorway 2

Nashua Yarn's *Creative Focus Worsted:* A = #3089 Blue Smoke, B = #1256 Soft Sage, C = #3812 Pale Violet, D = #0734 Natural Heather, E = #3915 Dusty Blue, F = #0100 Natural, G = #2380 Oatmeal, H = #1837 Soft Pink, I = #1460 Juniper, J = #0282 Taupe Heather, and K = #4053 Lavender

A = #1450 Blue Pine, B = #0117 Grass, C = #4899 Khaki, D = #1410 Emerald, E = #1460 Juniper, F = #1265 New Fern, G = #3360 Teal, H = #1256 Soft Sage, I = #1355 Pine, J = #3112 Evergreen, and K = #0715 Light Olive Heather

WRAP

With A, cast on 289 stitches.

Change to B, begin in linen stitch, and work even in the Stripe Pattern, changing color every row, until the piece measures approximately 25"/[63.5cm] from the beginning, ending after 1 row worked with A.

Bind off with A.

FINISHING

With the right side facing, attach additional strands of matching fringe (page 135) to the 2 shorter sides of wrap, matching colors.

Trim the fringe evenly.

scrap happy

Each one-row stripe uses approximately 6½ yd/[6m] of yarn.

DIY | *altered dimensions*

It would be simple to use this beautiful stitch pattern to create a warm econo-throw! Start your piece with 307 stitches for a 68"/[172.5cm] size afghan. Note: Try this noncurling fabric in other sizes—and in machine-washable yarns—for place mats, too. When one side gets crumbs on it, presto change-o!, just flip it over. The place mat will look different—but still attractive—on the other side!

strathaven

If you've already made lots of sweaters for your favorite guy, you're sure to have enough yarn—and in just the right colors!—languishing in your stash. Dig some out and get knitting!

SKILL LEVEL
Intermediate

SIZES
Small (Medium, Large, X-Large, XX-Large, XXX-Large). Instructions are for the smallest size, with changes for other sizes noted in parentheses as necessary.

FINISHED MEASUREMENTS
Chest: 43 (47, 50, 54, 57½, 61)"/[109, 119.5, 127, 137, 146, 155)cm]
Length: 26½ (26½, 27, 27½, 28, 28)"/[67.5 (67.5, 68.5, 70, 71, 71)cm]

MATERIALS
- Medium/worsted weight yarn (4)
  - 220 (235, 250, 270, 290, 310) yd/[201 (215, 228.5, 247, 265, 283.5)m] in the ribbing color (A)
  - 175 (190, 205, 220, 240, 255) yd/[160 (173.5, 187.5, 201, 219.5, 233)m] in each of 4 contrast colors (B, C, E, and G)
  - 75 (85, 90, 100, 110, 115) yd/[68.5 (77.5, 82.5, 91.5, 100.5, 105)m] in each of 3 other contrast colors (D, H, and J)
  - 140 (150, 160, 170, 190, 200) yd/[128 (137, 146.5, 155.5, 173.5, 183)m] in each of 2 other contrast colors (F and I)

- Size 7 [4.5mm] knitting needles
- Size 9 [5.5mm] knitting needles, or size needed to obtain gauge
- 1 safety pin
- Blunt-end yarn needle
- 1 stitch marker

The sample project uses Mission Falls' 1824 Wool (4-medium/worsted weight; 100% merino superwash wool; each approximately 1¾ oz/[50g] and 85 yd/ [78m]): #017 Heath (A), #023 Amethyst (B), #011 Poppy (C), #022 Ink (D), #024 Damson (E), #029 Raspberry (F), #021 Denim (G), #003 Oyster (H), #004 Charcoal (I), and #0534 Rhubarb (J)

GAUGE
18 stitches and 18 rows = 4"/[10cm] in stockinette stitch with the larger needles.
To save time, take time to check gauge.

NOTES
- Use the stranded technique (pages 133–134) for the colorwork.
- To decrease, use k2tog (page 130) at the beginning of a row and ssk (page 132) at the end of a row.
- To increase, use the M1 knitwise technique page 131).

STITCH PATTERNS

Rib Pattern (multiple of 2 stitches)
PATTERN ROW: *K1, p1; repeat from the * across.

Fair Isle Pattern, Rows 1–44
See the chart.

Fair Isle Pattern, Rows 45–88
See the chart.

Stockinette Stitch (any number of stitches)
ROW 1 (RS): Knit across.
ROW 2: Purl across.
Repeat Rows 1 and 2 for the pattern.

Alternative Colorway 1

Mission Falls' *1824 Wool*: A = #012 Raisin, B = #028 Pistachio, C = #017 Heath, D = #014 Dijon, E = #013 Curry, F = #010 Russet, G = #009 Nectar, H = #002 Stone, I = #008 Earth, and J = #531 Sprout

Alternative Colorway 2

A = #019 Mist, B = #027 Macaw, C = #018 Spruce, D = #001 Natural, E = #531 Sprout, F = #030 Teal, G = #003 Oyster, H = #536 Aster, I = #028 Pistachio, and J = #021 Denim

BACK

With the smaller needles and B, cast on 90 (96, 102, 110, 116, 124) stitches.

Begin the Rib Pattern, and work one row.

Change to A, and purl across.

Continue the Rib Pattern with A until the piece measures approximately 2½"/[6.5cm] from the beginning, ending after a wrong-side row and increasing 7 (9, 11, 11, 13, 13) stitches evenly across the last row—97 (105, 113, 121, 129, 137) stitches.

Change to the larger needles, begin Row 1 of the Fair Isle Pattern where indicated for your size, and work even in the pattern until the piece measures approximately 16½"/[42cm] from the beginning, ending after a wrong-side row.

Shape Armholes

Bind off 6 (7, 8, 9, 10, 11) stitches at the beginning of the next 2 rows; bind off 4 (4, 5, 6, 6, 6) stitches at the beginning of the next 2 rows; decrease 1 stitch at each side every row 8 (9, 10, 11, 12, 12) times, then every other row once—59 (63, 65, 67, 71, 77) stitches remain.

Continue even in the pattern as established until the piece measures approximately 25 (25, 25½, 26, 26½, 26½)"/[63.5 (63.5, 65, 66, 67.5, 67.5)cm] from the beginning, ending after a wrong-side row.

Shape Neck

Work the pattern as established across the first 13 (15, 16, 17, 19, 22) stitches; join a second ball of yarn and bind off the center 33 stitches; work the pattern across to end the row.

Work both sides at once with separate balls of yarn and decrease 1 stitch at each neck edge once—12 (14, 15, 16, 18, 21) stitches remain on each side.

Continue even until the piece measures approximately 25½ (25½, 26, 26½, 27, 27)"/[65 (65, 66, 67.5, 68.5, 68.5)cm] from the beginning, ending after a wrong-side row.

Shape Shoulders

Bind off 6 (7, 8, 8, 9, 11) stitches at the beginning of the next 2 rows, then bind off 6 (7, 7, 8, 9, 10) stitches at the beginning of the next 2 rows.

FRONT

Work the same as the Back until the piece measures approximately 17 (17, 17½, 18, 18½, 18½)"/[43 (43, 44.5, 45.5, 47, 47)cm] from the beginning, ending with a wrong-side row.

Shape Neck

Continue the armhole shaping same as for the back, *and at the same time,* slip the center stitch onto a safety pin.

Continue the pattern as established, and decrease 1 stitch at each neck edge every other row 15 times, then every fourth row twice—12 (14, 15, 16, 18, 21) stitches remain.

Continue even in the pattern until the piece measures the same as the back to the shoulders.

Shape Shoulders

Work the same as for the back.

FINISHING

Darn in all remaining yarn tails (page 135).

Block both pieces to the finished measurements (page 135).

Sew the left shoulder seam.

Neckband

With the right side facing, smaller needles, and A, begin at the Back right shoulder edge, and pick up and knit 44 stitches along the back of the neck, 41 stitches along the left front neck edge, 1 stitch from the safety pin, and 40 stitches along the right front neck edge—126 stitches total. Place a marker on the center front stitch.

NEXT ROW (WS): *P1, k1; repeat from the * across.
NEXT ROW: Work the pattern as established across to 2 stitches before the marked stitch, ssk, knit the center stitch, k2tog, continue the pattern as established across to end the row.
NEXT ROW: Work the pattern as established across to 2 stitches

before the marked stitch, p2tog, purl the center stitch, ssp, continue the pattern as established across to end the row.

NEXT ROW: Change to B; knit across to 2 stitches before the marked stitches, ssk, knit the center stitch, k2tog, knit across to end the row.
NEXT ROW: Work the pattern as established across to 2 stitches before the marked stitch, p2tog, purl the center stitch, ssp, continue the pattern as established across to end the row.
NEXT ROW: Bind off *loosely* in the pattern.

Sew the right shoulder seam, including the side of the neckband.

Armband

With the right side facing, smaller needles, and A, begin at the beginning of the front armhole shaping, pick up and knit 104 (104, 110, 116, 122, 122) stitches along the armhole.

Begin the Rib Pattern, and work even until the armband measures approximately 1"/[2.5cm] from the beginning, ending after a wrong-side row.

NEXT ROW (RS): Change to B, and knit across.

Bind off *loosely* in the pattern.

Sew the side seams, including the side of the armbands.

scrap happy

If your stash only allows one patterned stripe out of a particular color, there's absolutely no reason you can't use new colors for each one! Try to maintain a cohesive color story (page 17) so the project doesn't look scrappy.

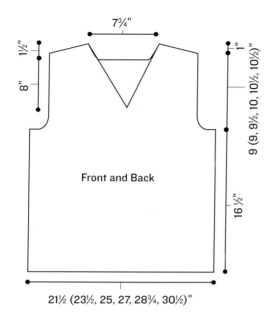

7¾"

1½"

8"

Front and Back

16½"

9 (9, 9½, 10, 10½, 10½)"

1"

21½ (23½, 25, 27, 28¾, 30½)"

Fair Isle Chart Rows 1–44

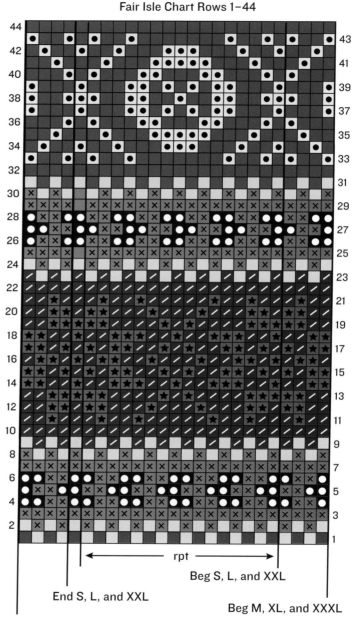

rpt

Beg S, L, and XXL

End S, L, and XXL

Beg M, XL, and XXXL

End M, XL, and XXXL

Fair Isle Chart Rows 45–88

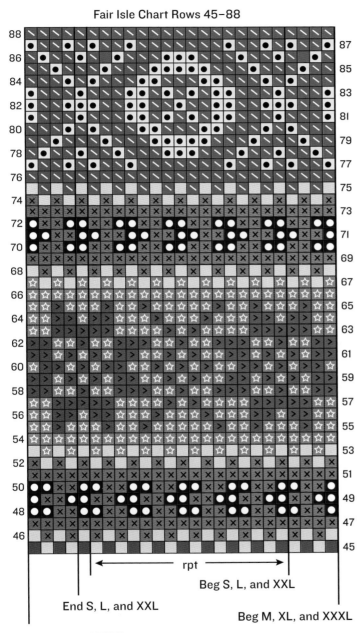

Color Key

- = A
- = B
- = C
- = D
- = E
- = F
- = G
- = H
- = I
- = J

Stitch Key

- = K on RS; p on WS

rpt

Beg S, L, and XXL

End S, L, and XXL

Beg M, XL, and XXXL

End M, XL, and XXXL

in the "thick" of it

five projects using chunky and bulky yarns

If you've got bunches of bulky yarn stowed in your stash, knit the projects in this chapter. Each one calls for chunky and bulky weight yarn (CYCA categories 5 and 6).

You don't have enough thick yarn to make one of the projects? Easy! Just combine strands of thinner yarn to achieve the gauge as described in the Bravissimo Throw (page 125). Refer to the chart on page 12 for more yarn combinations that will work for this gauge.

urban knitster slouch hat

Who ever said that keeping warm had to look ho-hum? Here's a winter hat that's anything but stodgy. It's such a quick knit that you can easily knock it out the morning of a bad-hair day.

SKILL LEVEL
Advanced Beginner

SIZE
Fits an average woman's head

FINISHED MEASUREMENT
Circumference: 18"/[45.5cm]

MATERIALS
- Bulky weight yarn (5)
  - 150 yd/[137m]
- Size 9 [5.5mm] circular knitting needle, 16"/[40cm] long
- Size 11 [8mm] circular knitting needle, 16"/[40cm] long, or size needed to obtain gauge
- Size 11 [8mm] double-pointed knitting needles (set of 5), or size needed to obtain gauge
- 1 stitch marker
- Blunt-end yarn needle

The sample project uses Brown Sheep Company's Lanaloft Bulky (5-bulky weight; 100% wool; each approximately 7 oz/[200g] and 160 yd/[146m]): #LL87 Catamaran Seas

GAUGE
10 stitches and 17 rounds = 4"/[10cm] in the Lace Pattern with the larger circular knitting needle.
To save time, take time to check gauge.

NOTES
- Constructionwise, this design is made in the round from the bottom up.
- When making the hat, change to double-pointed needles when there are too few stitches remaining to knit comfortably with the circular needle.

STITCH PATTERNS
Rib Pattern (multiple of 2 stitches)
ROUND 1 (RS): *K1, p1; repeat from the * around.
Repeat Round 1 for the pattern.

Lace Pattern (multiple of 13 stitches)
ROUND 1: *K1, yarn over, k2, ssk, k4, k2tog, k2, yarn over; repeat from the * around.
ROUND 2 AND ALL EVEN-NUMBERED ROUNDS: Knit.
ROUND 3: *K2, yarn over, k2, ssk, k2, k2tog, k2, yarn over, k1; repeat from the * around.
ROUND 5: *K3, yarn over, k2, ssk, k2tog, k2, yarn over, k2; repeat from the * around.
ROUND 6: Knit.

Repeat Rounds 1–6 for the pattern.
Or see the chart.

Alternative Colorway 1

Brown Sheep Company's *Lanaloft Bulky*: #BLL777 Autumn Run

Alternative Colorway 2

#LL85 Dark Magenta

HAT

With the smaller circular knitting needle, cast on 52 stitches.

Place a marker on the needle to indicate the beginning of the round and join, being careful not to twist the stitches on the needle; slip the marker every round.

Begin the Rib Pattern and work even until the piece measures

marker, k2tog, repeat ⌐
times more, then knit to the end of the round—12 stitches decreased.

NEXT ROUND: Knit around.
Repeat the last 2 rounds twice more—42 stitches remain.
Repeat the Decrease Round twice more—18 stitches remain.

LAST ROUND: Removing the markers, *k1, ssk; repeat from the * around—12 stitches remain.
Do not bind off.

Break the yarn, leaving a 6"/[15cm] tail. Thread the tail through the remaining stitches and pull it tight to secure.

Fasten off.

FINISHING

Darn in all remaining yarn tails (page 135).

Block the piece to the finished measurements (page 135).

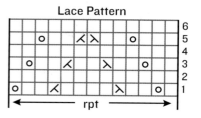

Lace Pattern

rpt

Stitch Key

☐ = K

o = Yarn over

⋋ = Ssk

⋌ = K2tog

rick rack

rick rack

This textured hat is a perfect project for that one extra ball of bulky yarn you have left over from another project. The simple cable pattern is easy to memorize—and quick to work. Jackpot!

SKILL LEVEL
Advanced Beginner

SIZES
Average woman's (man's) head. Instructions are for the smaller size, with changes for the other size noted in parentheses as necessary.

FINISHED MEASUREMENT
Circumference: 18 (19½)"/[45.5 (49.5)cm]

MATERIALS
- Bulky/chunky weight yarn 🄻
  - 85 (100) yd/[78 (91.5)m]
- Size 11 [8mm] circular knitting needle, 16"/[40cm] long, or size needed to obtain gauge
- Size 11 [8mm] double-pointed knitting needles (set of 5), or size needed to obtain gauge
- 1 stitch marker
- 1 cable needle
- Blunt-end yarn needle

The sample project uses Malabrigo Yarn's Chunky *(5-bulky/chunky weight; 100% merino wool; each approximately 3½ oz/[100g] and 104 yd/[95m]): #242 Intenso for the woman's version and #23 Pagoda for the man's version)*

GAUGE
14 stitches and 16 rounds = 4"/[10cm] in the Rick Rack Pattern. *To save time, take time to check gauge.*

NOTES
- Constructionwise, this design is made in the round from the bottom up.
- When making the hat, change to double-pointed needles when there are too few stitches remaining to knit comfortably with the circular needle.

STITCH PATTERN
Rick Rack Pattern (multiple of 5 stitches)
ROUND 1: *Slip 1 stitch onto a cn and hold in front, k2, k1 from the cn, p2; repeat from the * around.
ROUND 2: *K3, p2; repeat from the * around.
ROUND 3: *Slip 2 stitches onto a cn and hold in back, k1, k2 from the cn, p2; repeat from the * around.
ROUND 4: As Round 2.
Repeat Rounds 1–4 for the pattern.
Or see the chart.

Alternative Colorway 1   Alternative Colorway 2

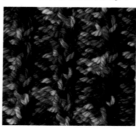   

Malabrigo Yarn's *Chunky*: #204 Oceanos   #56 Olive

HAT

With the circular knitting needle, cast on 60 (65) stitches.

Place a marker on the needle to indicate the beginning of the round and join, being careful not to twist the stitches on the needle; slip the marker every round.

Begin the Rick Rack Pattern and work even until the piece measures approximately 6½ (7½)"/[16.5 (19) cm] from the beginning, ending after Round 4 of the pattern.

Shape Crown

NEXT ROUND (DECREASE ROUND): *Slip the next stitch onto a cn and hold it in front of the work, k2, then slip the stitch from the cn back onto the left-hand needle, ssk to combine the knit stitch and the purl stitch, p1; repeat from the * around—48 (52) stitches remain.

NEXT ROUND: *K3, p1; repeat from the * around.

NEXT ROUND: *Slip the next 2 stitches onto a cn and hold them in back of the work, k1, knit the 2 stitches on the cn, p1; repeat from the * around.

NEXT ROUND: *K3, p1; repeat from the * around.

NEXT ROUND (DECREASE ROUND): *Slip the next stitch onto a cn and hold it in front of the work, k2, then slip the stitch from the cn back onto the left-hand needle, ssk to combine the knit stitch and the purl stitch; repeat from the * around—36 (39) stitches remain.

NEXT ROUND: Knit to the end of the round, remove the marker, k2, replace marker for new beginning of the round.

NEXT ROUND: *Ssk, k1; repeat from the * around—24 (26) stitches remain.

NEXT ROUND: Ssk around—12 (13) stitches remain.
Do not bind off.

Break the yarn, leaving a 6"/[15cm] tail. Thread the tail through the remaining stitches and pull it tight to secure.

Fasten off.

FINISHING

Darn in all remaining yarn tails (page 135).

Block the piece to the finished measurements (page 135).

Rick Rack Pattern

Stitch Key

☐ = K

• = P

✕ = Slip 2 stitches onto cn and hold in back; k1; k2 from cn

✕ = Slip next st onto cn and hold in front; k2; k1 from cn

hot yet cool cardi

Believe it or not, you can make this sweater in just one fun weekend of marathon knitting! Since it's worked from the top down, you can try it on as you go, making choices like sleeve and body length easy to best suit you.

SKILL LEVEL
Advanced Beginner

SIZES
X-Small (Small, Medium, Large, 1X, 2X). Instructions are for the smallest size, with changes for other sizes noted in parentheses as necessary.

FINISHED MEASUREMENTS
Bust (*buttoned*): 35 (38³/₄, 42¹/₂, 43³/₄, 46¹/₄, 48)"/[89 (98.5, 108, 111, 117.5, 122)cm]
Length: 13 (14, 15¹/₄, 15¹/₂, 16¹/₄, 17)"/[33 (35.5, 38.5, 39.5, 41.5, 43)cm]

MATERIALS
- Bulky/chunky weight yarn (5)
  - 170 (205, 245, 260, 285, 315) yd/[155.5 (187.5, 224, 238, 261, 288)m] in the main color (A)
  - 19 (23, 28, 29, 32, 35) yd/[17.5 (21, 26, 26.5, 29.5, 32) m] in each of 9 contrasting colors (B, C, D, E, F, G, H, I, and J)
- Size 10¹/₂ [6.5mm] circular knitting needle, 40"/ [100cm] long, or size needed to obtain gauge
- Size 10¹/₂ [6.5mm] double-pointed needles (set of 4)
- 4 stitch markers
- 2 stitch holders (optional)
- One 1¹/₂"/[38mm] button (One World Button Supply Company's *SPN 106-44 CN* was used on the sample garment)
- Blunt-end yarn needle

The sample project uses Cascade Yarn's 128 Chunky Solid (5-bulky/chunky weight; 100% Peruvian Highland wool; each approximately 3¹/₂ oz/[100g] and 128 yd/[117m]): #9465B Pumpkin (A), #7822 Bark (B), #9466 Scarlet (C), #8686 Chocolate (D), #9404 Deep Red (E), #2414 Toffee (F), #2401 Shiraz (G), #9408 Red Oak (H), #9474 Lipstick Mauve (I), and #2411 Brick (J)

GAUGE
13 stitches = 4"/[10cm] and 32 rows = 6"/[15cm] in the Garter Ridge Pattern.
To save time, take time to check gauge.

NOTES
- This garment is made from the top down in one piece.
- Always knit the first and last stitch of every row.

STITCH PATTERNS
Garter Ridge Pattern—flat (any number of stitches)
ROW 1 (RS): With A, knit across.
ROW 2: With A, knit across.
ROW 3: With a contrasting color, knit across.
ROW 4: With a contrasting color, purl across.
Repeat Rows 1–4 for the pattern.

Garter Ridge Pattern—circular (any number of stitches)

ROUND 1: With A, knit around.
ROUND 2: With A, purl around.
ROUNDS 3 AND 4: With a contrasting color, knit around.
Repeat Rounds 1–4 for the pattern.

Stripe Pattern

Work *2 rows with A, 2 rows with B, 2 rows with A, 2 rows with C, 2 rows with A, 2 rows with D, 2 rows with A, 2 rows with E, 2 rows with A, 2 rows with F, 2 rows with A, 2 rows with G, 2 rows with A, 2 rows with H, 2 rows with A, 2 rows with I, 2 rows with A, 2 rows with J; repeat from the * for the pattern.

Cascade Yarn's 128 *Chunky Solid*:
A = #9430 Lawn Green, B = #8910 Light Spring Green, C = #2452 Meadow, D = #8267 Bottle Green, E = #8903 Lime, F = #9429 Dark Loden, G = #9464B Avocado, H = #8914 Frog, I = #9338 Heather Green, and J = #9448 Forest

A = #9474 Lipstick Mauve, B = #8400 Charcoal, C = #8393 Admiral Navy, D = #8886 Eggplant, E = #8561 Gray Teal, F = #8885 Grape, G = #9548 Blue Gray, H = #9554 Sky, I = #4002 Dark Charcoal, and J = #9541 Lilac

CARDI

With circular needle and A, use the cable cast on technique (page 000) to cast on 66 stitches.

ROW 1 (RS): K11 for right front, yarn over, place marker, k1, yarn over, k10 for right sleeve, yarn over, place marker, k1, yarn over, k20 for back, yarn over, place marker, k1, yarn over, k10 for left sleeve, yarn over, place marker, k1, yarn over, k11 for left front—74 stitches.
ROW 2: K1, yarn over (for buttonhole), k2tog, knit across to the end of the row.
ROW 3: Change color; *knit across to the next marker, yarn over, slip marker, k1, yarn over; repeat from the * 3 more times, knit across to the end of the row—82 stitches.
ROW 4: K1, purl across to the last stitch, k1.
ROW 5: Change color; *knit across to the next marker, yarn over, slip marker, k1, yarn over; repeat from the * 3 more times, knit across to the end of the row—90 stitches.
ROW 6: Knit across to the end of the row.

Repeat [Rows 3–6] 7 (8, 10, 10, 11, 12) times, then work [Rows 3 and 4] 0 (1, 0, 1, 1, 1) time—202 (226, 250, 258, 274, 290) stitches.

Divide Body and Sleeves

NEXT ROW (RS): Change color; removing markers as you go, k29 (32, 35, 36, 38, 40) stitches, slip the next 44 (50, 56, 58, 62, 66) stitches onto a holder or piece of scrap yarn for the right sleeve, k56 (62, 68, 70, 74, 78) stitches, slip the next 44 (50, 56, 58, 62, 66) stitches onto a holder or piece of scrap yarn for the left sleeve, k29 (32, 35, 36, 38, 40) front stitches to end the row—114 (126, 138, 142, 150, 158) stitches.

BODY

NEXT ROW (WS): K1, knit across 112 (124, 136, 140, 148, 156) stitches of the body, k1—114 (126, 138, 142, 150, 158) stitches.

Continue even in the patterns as established until the piece measures approximately 4½"/ [11.5cm] from the dividing row, ending after 2 rows are worked with a contrast color.

Lower Border

Change to A and knit 4 rows.

Bind off.

RIGHT SLEEVE

Slip the 44 (50, 56, 58, 62, 66) right sleeve stitches from the holder to 3 double-pointed needles.

With the right side facing and the next color in the Stripe Pattern, knit around, then place a marker for the beginning of the round and join.

Continue working the Garter Ridge and Stripe patterns as established and *at the same time,* on the first round with contrasting color, decrease 6 (7, 7, 8, 8, 9) stitches evenly around—38 (43, 49, 50, 54, 57) stitches remain.

Continue even in the patterns as established until the piece measures approximately 1"/[2.5cm] from the dividing row, ending after 2 rounds worked with a contrast color.

Lower Border
Change to A; [knit 1 round, purl 1 round] twice.

Bind off.

LEFT SLEEVE
Work the same as the right sleeve.

FINISHING
Darn in all remaining yarn tails (page 135).

Block the piece to the finished measurements (page 135).

Sew on button opposite the buttonhole.

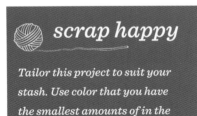

scrap happy

Tailor this project to suit your stash. Use color that you have the smallest amounts of in the upper yoke, as those rows are the shortest.

| DIY | *the long and the short of it* |

If you'd prefer a longer, more traditional look, just add more rows after the dividing row.

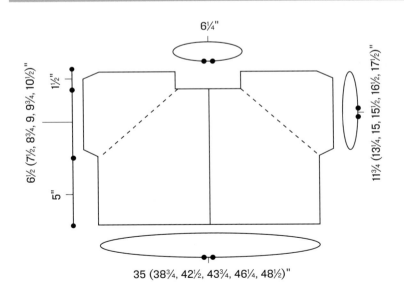

6¼"

1½"

6½ (7½, 8¾, 9, 9¾, 10½)"

5"

11¾ (13¾, 15, 15½, 16½, 17½)"

35 (38¾, 42½, 43¾, 46¼, 48½)"

amy's sleeveless hoodie

I bet no one will ever guess that you knitted this piece using yarn scraps! A few skeins of a main color creates a cohesive look. The hood makes it especially cozy to wear.

SKILL LEVEL
Intermediate

SIZES
Small (Medium, Large, 1X, 2X, 3X). Instructions are for the smallest size, with changes for other sizes noted in parentheses as necessary.

FINISHED MEASUREMENTS
Bust (zipped): 35$\frac{1}{2}$ (39$\frac{1}{2}$, 43$\frac{1}{2}$, 47$\frac{1}{2}$, 51$\frac{1}{2}$, 55$\frac{1}{2}$)"/[90 (100.5, 110.5, 121, 131, 141)cm]
Length: 25"/[63.5cm]

MATERIALS
- Bulky/chunky weight yarn ⑤
  - 375 (395, 410, 420, 435, 445) yd/[343 (361, 375, 384, 398, 407)m] in the main color (A)
  - 60 (65, 70, 70, 75, 80) yd/[55 (59.5, 64, 64, 68.5, 73)m] in each of 12 contrasting colors (B, C, D, E, F, G, H, I, J, K, L, and M)
- Size 13 [9mm] knitting needles, or size needed to obtain gauge
- Size 13 [9mm] circular knitting needle, 24"/[60cm] long, or size needed to obtain gauge
- Size 13 [9mm] circular knitting needle, 16"/[40cm] long
- Size 13 [9mm] double-pointed knitting needles (set of 4), or size needed to obtain gauge
- 12 stitch markers
- 4 stitch holders
- Blunt-end yarn needle
- One 22"/[55cm] long separating zipper
- Pins
- Contrasting sewing thread
- Matching sewing thread
- Sharp sewing needle

Sample project uses Brown Sheep Company's Lamb's Pride Bulky (5-bulky/chunky weight; 85% wool/15% mohair; each approximately 4 oz/[113g] and 125 yd/[114.5m]): #M89 Roasted Coffee (A), #M164 Brown Bear (B), #M140 Aran (C), #M02 Brown Heather (D), #M116 Camel Back (E), #M08 Wild Oak (F), #M193 Bittersweet (G), #M10 Creme (H), #M151 Chocolate Souffle (I), #M185 Aubergine (J), #M115 Oatmeal (K), #M07 Sable (L), and #M01 Sandy Heather (M)

GAUGE
12 stitches and 24 rows = 4"/[10cm] in the Tweed Pattern.
To save time, take time to check gauge.

NOTES
- Always slip stitches purlwise (page 132) with the working yarn held to the wrong side of the fabric (to the back on RS rows and to the front on WS rows)
- One selvedge stitch has been added on each side of the fabric; these stitches are not reflected in the final measurements.
- To decrease, use k2tog (page 130) at the beginning of a row and ssk (page 132) at the end of a row.

Tweed Pattern (multiple of 3 + 1 stitches)

ROW 1 (RS): Change color; k3, *slip the next stitch, k2; repeat from the * across, ending the row with k1.

ROW 2: K3, *slip the next stitch, k2; repeat from the * across, ending the row with k1.

ROW 3: Change color; *k2, slip the next stitch; repeat from the * across, ending the row with k1.

ROW 4: K1, *slip the next stitch, k2; repeat from the * across.

ROW 5: Change color; k1, *slip the next stitch, k2; repeat from the * across.

ROW 6: *K2, slip the next stitch; repeat from the * across, ending row with k1.

Repeat Rows 1–6 for the pattern.

Stripe Pattern

Work *2 rows with B, 2 rows with C, 2 rows with D, 2 rows with A, 2 rows with E, 2 rows with F, 2 rows with G, 2 rows with A, 2 rows with H, 2 rows with I, 2 rows with J, 2 rows with A, 2 rows with K, 2 rows with L, 2 rows with M, 2 rows with A; repeat from the * for the pattern.

Stockinette Stitch (any number of stitches)

ROW 1 (RS): Knit across.

ROW 2: Purl across.

Repeat Rows 1 and 2 for the pattern.

Alternative Colorway 1   Alternative Colorway 2

Brown Sheep Company's *Lamb's Pride Bulky*: A = #M75 Blue Heirloom, B = #M190 Jaded Dreams, C = #M187 Turquoise Depths, D = #M79 Blue Boy, E = #M120 Limeade, F = #M57 Brite Blue, G = #M78 Aztec Turquoise, H = #M16 Seafoam, I = #M165 Christmas Green, J = #1M92 Caribbean Waves, K= #M191 Kiwi, L = #M82 Blue Flannel, M = #M51 Winter Blue

A = #M38 Lotus Pink, B = #M174 Wild Mustard, C = #M23 Fuchsia, D = #M22 Autumn Harvest, E = #M34 Victorian Pink, F = #M155 Lemon Drop, G = #M105 RPM Pink, H = #M110 Orange You Glad, I = #M183 Rosado Rose, J = #M14 Sunburst Gold, K = #M97 Rust, L = #M162 Mulberry, and M = #M102 Orchid Thistle

BACK

With A, cast on 55 (61, 67, 73, 79, 85) stitches.

Knit one row.

Change to B; begin the Tweed Pattern in the Stripe Pattern, and work even until the piece measures approximately 16 1/4 (15 3/4, 15 1/4, 14 3/4, 14 3/4, 14 3/4)"/[41.5 (40, 38.5, 37.5, 37.5, 37.5)cm] from the beginning, ending after a wrong-side row.

Shape Armholes

Bind off 3 (4, 5, 6, 7, 8) stitches at the beginning of the next 2 rows; bind off 2 (2, 3, 3, 4, 4) stitches at the beginning of the next 2 rows; decrease 1 stitch at each side every row 0 (0, 0, 0, 0, 2) times, every other row 1 (4, 3, 6, 6, 7) times, then every fourth row 2 (1, 2, 1, 1, 0) times—39 (39, 41, 41, 43, 43) stitches remain.

Continue even in the pattern until the piece measures approximately 24"/[61cm] from the beginning, ending after a wrong-side row.

Shape Shoulders

Bind off 3 (3, 4, 4, 4, 4) stitches at the beginning of the next 4 rows, then bind off 4 (4, 3, 3, 4, 4) stitches at the beginning of the next 2 rows— 19 stitches remain.

Bind off.

POCKET LINING (MAKE 2)

With A, cast on 16 (17, 16, 17, 16, 17) stitches.

Begin in stockinette stitch and work even until the piece measures approximately 4 1/2"/[11.5cm] from the beginning, ending after a wrong-side row.

Slip the stitches onto a holder.

LEFT FRONT

With A, cast on 28 (31, 34, 37, 40, 43) stitches.

Knit one row.

Change to B; begin the Tweed Pattern in the Stripe Pattern, and work even until the piece measures approximately 5"/[12.5cm] from the beginning, ending after a wrong-side row.

Place Pockets
Work across the first 6 (7, 9, 10, 12, 13) stitches; slip the next 16 (17, 16, 17, 16, 17) stitches onto holder; with the right side facing, work across 16 (17, 16, 17, 16, 17) stitches from one pocket lining holder; work across to end the row.

Continue even in the pattern as established until the piece measures approximately 16¼"/[41.5cm] from the beginning, ending after a wrong-side row.

Shape Armhole
Bind off 3 (4, 5, 6, 7, 8) stitches at the armhole edge once; bind off 2 (2, 3, 3, 4, 4) stitches at the armhole edge once; decrease 1 stitch at the armhole edge every row 0 (0, 0, 0, 0, 2) times, every other row 1 (4, 3, 6, 6, 7) times, then every fourth row 2 (1, 2, 1, 1, 0) times—20 (20, 21, 21, 22, 22) stitches remain.

Continue even in the pattern until the piece measures approximately 22"/[56cm] from the beginning, ending after a right-side row.

Shape Neck
NEXT ROW (WS): Work the pattern as established across the first 5 stitches and slip them onto a holder, then work the pattern as established across to end the row—15 (15, 16, 16, 17, 17) stitches remain. *Make a note of which row of the pattern you ended with as well as the color used for this row.*

Bind off 2 stitches at the neck edge twice, then decrease 1 stitch at the neck edge once—10 (10, 11, 11, 12, 12) stitches remain.

Continue even until the piece measures the same as the back to the shoulders, ending after a wrong-side row.

Shape Shoulders
Bind off 3 (3, 4, 4, 4, 4) stitches at the armhole edge twice.

Work one row even—4 (4, 3, 3, 4, 4) stitches remain.

Bind off.

RIGHT FRONT
With A, cast on 28 (31, 34, 37, 40, 43) stitches.

Knit one row.

Change to B; begin the Tweed Pattern in the Stripe Pattern and work even until the piece measures approximately 5"/[12.5cm] from the beginning, ending after a wrong-side row.

Place Pockets
Work across first 6 (7, 9, 10, 12, 13) stitches; slip the next 16 (17, 16, 17, 16, 17) stitches onto holder; with the right side facing, work across 16 (17, 16, 17, 16, 17) stitches from one pocket lining holder; work across to end the row.

Continue even in the pattern as established until the piece measures approximately 16¼"/[41.5cm] from the beginning, ending after a right-side row.

Shape Armhole
Bind off 3 (4, 5, 6, 7, 8) stitches at the armhole edge once; bind off 2 (2, 3, 3, 4, 4) stitches at the armhole edge once; decrease 1 stitch at the armhole edge every row 0 (0, 0, 0, 0, 2) times, every other row 1 (4, 3, 6, 6, 7) times, then every fourth row 2 (1, 2, 1, 1, 0) times—20 (20, 21, 21, 22, 22) stitches remain.

Continue even in the pattern until the piece measures approximately 22"/[56cm] from the beginning, ending after the wrong-side row that is one row earlier than where you ended the Left Front before neck shaping (refer to your notes).

Shape Neck
NEXT ROW (RS): Work the pattern as established across the first 5 stitches and slip them onto a holder, then work pattern as established across to end the row—15 (15, 16, 16, 17, 17) stitches remain.

Bind off 2 stitches at the neck edge twice, then decrease 1 stitch at the neck edge once—10 (10, 11, 11, 12, 12) stitches remain.

Continue even until the piece measures the same as the back to the shoulders, ending after a wrong-side row.

Shape Shoulders
Bind off 3 (3, 4, 4, 4, 4) stitches at the armhole edge twice.

Work one row even—4 (4, 3, 3, 4, 4) stitches remain.

Bind off.

FINISHING
Darn in all remaining yarn tails (page 135).

Block all pieces to the finished measurements (page 135).

Pocket Edging

With the right side facing and A, pick up and knit 16 (17, 16, 17, 16, 17) stitches from one lining holder.

NEXT ROW (WS): Knit across.
NEXT ROW: Purl across.
NEXT ROW: Knit as you bind off.

Repeat for the second pocket edging.

Sew the sides of the pocket edgings to the Front.

Sew the pocket linings to the wrong side of the Front.

Sew the shoulder seams.

Sew the side seams.

Hood

With the right side facing, circular needle, and the same color you used on the first row of the Front neck shaping, pick up and knit 5 stitches from the Right Front stitch holder, 22 stitches along the Right Front neck, 19 stitches along the Back neck, 22 stitches along the Left Front neck, and 5 stitches from the Left Front stitch holder—73 stitches total.

NEXT ROW (WS): Using the same color as the pick-up row, k35, place a marker, k3, place marker, k35. Begin the Tweed Pattern in the Stripe Pattern *with the row after the one noted at the Left Front neck shaping*, and work even for 6 rows.
NEXT ROW (RS): Continue the patterns as established across to the first marker, slip the marker, M1 knit-wise (page 131), k3, M1 knitwise, slip the next marker, continue the patterns as established across to end of the row—75 stitches.

NEXT 7 ROWS: Continue the patterns as established across to the first marker, slip the marker, k5, slip the marker, continue the patterns as established across to end of the row.
NEXT ROW (RS): Continue the patterns as established across to the first marker, slip the marker, M1 knitwise, k5, M1 knitwise, slip the next marker, continue the patterns as established across to end of the row—77 stitches.
NEXT 7 ROWS: Continue the patterns as established across to the first marker, slip the marker, k7, slip the marker, continue the patterns as established across to end of the row.
NEXT ROW (RS): Continue the patterns as established across to the first marker, slip the marker, M1

knitwise, k7, M1 knitwise, slip the next marker, continue the patterns as established across to end of the row—79 stitches.
NEXT ROW: Continue the patterns as established across to the first marker, slip the marker, k9, slip the marker, continue the patterns as established across to end of the row. Work even in the patterns as established until the hood measures approximately 12"/[30.5cm] from the beginning, ending after a wrong-side row.

NEXT ROW (RS): Continue the patterns as established across to the first marker, slip the marker, k1, ssk, k3, k2tog, k1, slip the next marker, work the patterns as established to end of the row—77 stitches.

NEXT ROW: Continue the patterns as established across to the first marker, slip the marker, k7, slip the marker, continue the patterns as established across to end of the row.

NEXT ROW (RS): Continue the patterns as established across to the first marker, slip the marker, ssk, k3, k2tog, slip the next marker, work the patterns as established to end of the row—75 stitches.

NEXT ROW: Continue the patterns as established across to the first marker, slip the marker, k5, slip the marker, continue the patterns as established across to end of the row.

NEXT ROW (RS): Continue the patterns as established across to the first marker, slip the marker, ssk, k1, k2tog, slip the next marker, work the patterns as established to end of the row—73 stitches.

NEXT ROW: Continue the patterns as established across to the first marker, slip the marker, k3, slip the marker, continue the patterns as established across to end of the row.

NEXT ROW (RS): Continue the patterns as established across to first marker, remove the marker, slip the next stitch knitwise, k2tog, pass the slipped stitch over, remove the next marker, work the patterns as established until 2 stitches remain in the row, ending the row with k2tog—70 stitches.

Divide the remaining stitches onto 2 double-pointed needles, putting 35 stitches onto each one, and with the right sides facing each other and A, use the three-needle bind-off (page 134) to seam the top of the Hood.

Front Edging

With the right side facing, circular needle, and A, begin at the lower Right Front edge, and pick up and knit 72 stitches along Right Front edge, 80 stitches along front of Hood, and 72 stitches along Left Front edge—224 stitches total.

NEXT ROW (WS): Slip the first stitch knitwise, knit across.

NEXT ROW: Slip the first stitch purlwise, purl across.

NEXT ROW: Slip the first stitch knitwise, then knit as you bind off.

Armhole Edging

With the right side facing, shorter circular needle, and A, begin at the bottom of the armhole, and pick up and knit 58 (62, 66, 70, 70, 70) stitches around the armhole, dividing stitches evenly between 3 needles.

Place a marker for the beginning of the round, and join.

Purl 2 rounds.

Bind off purlwise.

Repeat for the other armhole.

Darn in all remaining yarn tails (page 135).

Sew in the zipper (page 136).

scrap happy

The sample garment uses one color as the main background color. For a completely different look, alternate two rows of every color throughout

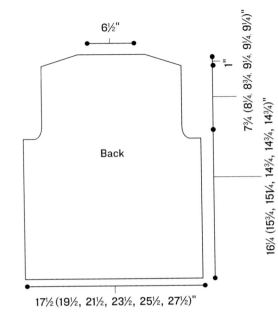

6½"

Back

7¾ (8¼, 8¾, 9¼, 9¼, 9¼)"

1"

16¼ (15¾, 15¼, 14¾, 14¾, 14¾)"

17½ (19½, 21½, 23½, 25½, 27½)"

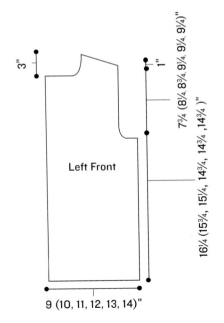

3"

Left Front

7¾ (8¼, 8¾, 9¼, 9¼, 9¼)"

1"

16¼ (15¾, 15¼, 14¾ , 14¾ , 14¾)"

9 (10, 11, 12, 13, 14)"

bravissimo throw

Combine various colors and textures to create this beautiful masterpiece.

SKILL LEVEL
Advanced Beginner

SIZE
One size

FINISHED MEASUREMENTS
48" x 60"/[122cm x 152.5cm]

MATERIALS
- Bulky/chunky weight yarn (5)
  - 612 yd/[560m] in the two main colors A and B
  - 40 yd/[37m] (or the equivalent if using a worsted-weight yarn doubled) for each stripe in several contrasting colors (C, D, E, F, G, H, I, J, K, L, M, N, and O)
- Size 11 [8mm] circular knitting needle, 36"/[90cm] long, or size needed to obtain gauge
- Blunt-end yarn needle

The sample project uses a variety of yarns from Plymouth Yarn:
- Baby Alpaca Grande (*5-bulky/chunky weight; 100% baby alpaca; each approximately 3½ oz/[100g] and 110 yd/[100.5m]): #809 Turquoise (A) and #3317 Pale Blue (H)*
- Baby Alpaca Grande Hand Dye (*5-bulky/chunky weight; 100% baby alpaca; each approximately 3¾ oz/[100g] and 110 yd/[100.5m]): #07 Teal (B)*
- Sinsation (*5-bulky/chunky weight; 80% rayon/20% wool; each approximately 1¾ oz/[50g] and 38 yd/[34.5m]): #3332 Plush Turquoise (C) and #3321 Sage (K)*
- Royal Llama Silk (*4-medium/worsted weight; 60% llama/40% silk; each approximately 1¾ oz/[50g] and 102 yd/[93.5m]): #1841 Teal (D)*
- Jeannee Worsted (*4-medium/worsted weight; 51% cotton/49% acrylic; each approximately 1¾ oz/ [50g] and 110 yd/[100.5m]) used with 2 strands held together: #18 Aqua (E) and #33 Bright Turquoise (N)*
- Drifting Gardens (*5-bulky/chunky weight; 72% mohair/16% wool/12% polyester; each approximately 1¾ oz/[50g] and 82 yd/[75m]): #201 Teal (F)*
- Fantasy Naturale (*4-medium/worsted weight; 100% mercerized cotton; each approximately 3½ oz/ [100g] and 140 yd/[128m]) used with 2 strands held together: #8017 Turquoise (G) and #9707 Turquoise Mix (L)*
- Refashion (*5-bulky/chunky weight; 68% recycled wool/5% recycled cashmere/23% nylon/4% rayon; each approximately 1¾ oz/[50g] and 104 yd/[95m]): #805 Blue Green (I)*
- Covington (*4-medium/worsted weight; 100% mercerized cotton; each approximately 3½ oz/[100g] and 184 yd/[168m]) used with 2 strands held together: #2005 Pale Aqua (J)*
- Taria Tweed (*5-bulky/chunky weight; 40% merino wool/30% llama/30% silk; each approximately 3½ oz/[100g] and 135 yd/[123.5m]): #2769 Deep Turquoise (M) and #2768 Light Turquoise (O)*

GAUGE

17 stitches and 11 rows = 4"/[10cm] in the Feather and Fan Ripple Pattern.

To save time, take time to check gauge.

NOTES

- The circular needle is used to accommodate the large number of stitches. Do not join at the end of rows, but rather, work back and forth in rows.
- This design calls for bulky weight yarn, but lighter weight yarns can be easily held together to create the appropriate weight of yarn (page 12). Here, 2 strands of worsted weight yarns are occasionally held together and act as one strand of bulky weight. When using multiple strands of a lighterweight yarn to create the equivalent of a bulky yarn, increase the yardage of that yarn appropriately.

STITCH PATTERNS

Border Pattern (multiple of 17 stitches)

ROW 1 (RS): *[K2tog] 3 times, [yarn over, k1] 5 times, yarn over, [ssk] 3 times; repeat from the * across.
ROW 2: Knit across.
Repeat Rows 1 and 2 for the pattern.

Feather and Fan Ripple Pattern (multiple of 17 stitches)

ROW 1 (RS): With B, *[K2tog] 3 times, [yarn over, k1] 5 times, yarn over, [ssk] 3 times; repeat from the * across.
ROW 2: Purl across.
ROWS 3–6: As Rows 1 and 2.
ROW 7: Change to a contrast color, work as Row 1.
ROW 8: Knit across.
ROWS 9–14: With A, same as Rows 1–6.
ROWS 15 AND 16: Change to a contrast color, same as Rows 7 and 8.
Repeat Rows 1–16 for the pattern.

Stripe Pattern

Work *6 rows with B, 2 rows with a contrast color, 6 rows with A, 2 rows with a contrast color; repeat from the * for the pattern.

Alternative Colorway 1

A = Plymouth Yarn's *Baby Alpaca Grande* in #2278 Mauve, B = #64 Light Steel, C = *Galway Worsted* worked with 2 strands held together in #98 Muted Lilac, D = Adriafil's *Capriccio* (5-bulky/chunky weight; 50% nylon/44% wool/6% polyester; each approximately 1³/₄ oz/[50g] and 65 yd/[59.5m]), #060 Mauve Mix, E = *Royal Llama Silk* in #1240 Lilac, F = *Taria Tweed* in #2763 Pink Tweed, G = *Fantasy Naturale* worked with 2 strands held together in #2576 Blue Gray, H = *Jeannee Worsted* worked with 2 strands held together in #23 Pale Lavender, I = *Covington* worked with 2 strands held together in #2011 Mauve, J = *Drifting Gardens* in #202 Mauve Mix

Alternative Colorway 2

A = Plymouth Yarn's *Baby Alpaca Grande* in #1285 Olive, B = *Baby Alpaca Grande Hand Dye* in #06 Autumn, C = *Galway Worsted* worked with 2 strands held together in #168 Toffee, D = *Refashion* #812 Autumnal Mix, E = *Royal Llama Silk* in #1880 Rust, F = *Taria Tweed* in #2760 Rust Tweed, G = *Fantasy Naturale* worked with 2 strands held together in #9420 Autumn Leaves, H = *Jeannee Worsted* worked with 2 strands held together in #30 Sage, I = *Covington* worked with 2 strands held together in #2018 Olive, J = *Drifting Gardens* in #204 Autumnal Mix

THROW

With A, cast on 204 stitches.

Begin the Border Pattern and work even for 6 rows.

Change to B, begin the Feather and Fan Ripple Pattern in the Stripe Pattern, and work even until the piece measures approximately 60"/[152.5cm] from the beginning, ending after 6 rows worked with B.

Change to A and work the Border Pattern for 6 rows.

Bind off in pattern.

FINISHING

Darn in all remaining yarn tails (page 135).

Block the piece to the finished measurements (page 135).

 scrap happy

Each 2-row stripe of contrast color uses about 20 yd/[18.5m] of yarn; each 6-row stripe of the two main colors uses about 54 yd/[49.5m] of yarn. (Medium yarns that have been doubled will require twice as much yardage.)

techniques

Obviously, everyone knits at different technical levels. This section provides instructions for many of the specific techniques used in the projects. If a particular design excites you but some of the techniques used in it seem unfamiliar, take a leap and please just go for it! Let your knitter's curiosity inspire you to learn new skills and grow.

KNITTING TECHNIQUES
(arranged alphabetically)

Attaching New Yarn

Whenever possible, try to attach a new ball of yarn at the beginning of a row.

To start a new color of yarn at the beginning of a knit row: Drop the old yarn, insert your right-hand needle into the first stitch of the row as if you are about to knit, grab the new yarn and use it to knit the first stitch (illustration 1). Always begin and end every yarn with at least a 6"/[15cm] tail. Otherwise, you won't have enough length to weave it in sufficiently.

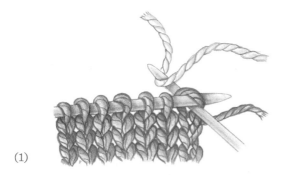

(1)

To start a new yarn at the beginning of a purl row: Drop the old yarn, insert your right-hand needle into that first stitch of the row as if you're about to purl rather than knit, and purl it.

Bobbles

Bobbles introduce wonderful surface texture (not to mention, playful whimsy) to fabrics. While some knitters find them time-consuming to knit, they are not difficult to do. To make a bobble, work several stitches into a single stitch, increasing the number of stitches in that area from one stitch to three, five, or more. Work several rows on these new stitches, turning the work after each successive row. Finally, decrease the stitches back to the original single stitch.

There are several ways to knit a bobble, but here's my favorite. It's used in Cables and Colors on page 87: Knit into the (front, back, front) of a single stitch, turn; working into these same 3 stitches, p1, (p1, yarn over, p1) *all into the next stitch*, then p1, turn; knit the 5 stitches, turn; decrease from 5 stitches down to 3 stitches as follows: P2tog, p1, p2tog, turn; Finally, decrease from 3 stitches down to 1 stitch as follows: slip 2 stitches at once knitwise, knit the next stitch, then pass the 2 slipped stitches from the right-hand needle over the last knit stitch as if you're binding them off.

Cables

Cables are created when stitches trade places with other stitches within a knitted row. One set of stitches is placed on a cable needle to keep them out of the way while another set of stitches is worked. Depending on whether those stitches are held to the front or to the back of the work, whether the cable uses two, three, or even seventeen stitches, and whether the stitches are ultimately knitted or purled or any combination of the two, you can create beautiful patterns. For a two-over-two right-crossed stockinette cable, for example, slip 2 stitches onto a cable needle and *hold them in back of the work;* knit 2 stitches from the left-hand needle, then knit the 2 stitches from cable needle. For a two-over-two left-crossed stockinette cable, slip 2 stitches onto a cable needle and *hold them in front of the work;* knit 2 stitches from the left-hand needle, then knit the 2 stitches from the cable needle.

Cable Cast-on

Here's my favorite cast-on technique: It's beautiful, easy, and quick to do. Plus, it's perfect when the first row worked is a right-side row.

Start by making a slip knot on your knitting needle, then insert the tip of the right-hand needle knitwise into the loop that's sitting on the left-hand needle and knit up a stitch (illustration 2) *but don't remove the original stitch from the left-hand needle;* instead, transfer the new stitch from the right-hand needle back to the left-hand one. One new stitch has been cast on.

For each successive stitch to be cast on, insert the tip of the right-hand needle *between* the first 2 stitches on the left-hand needle to knit up a stitch (illustration 3).

As before, do not remove the old stitch, rather slip the new one back onto the left-hand needle; repeat until you have cast on the required number of stitches.

Fasten Off

To finish a piece of fabric securely once the knitting is completed, cut the yarn, leaving a tail at least 6"/[15cm] long, and fasten off by drawing the loose tail through the remaining stitch on the knitting needle. Later, this yarn tail can be used for seaming or else must be woven in (see page 135).

Intarsia

This type of colorwork technique is used to draw pictures in knitted fabric and often require several balls of yarn across each row, one for each section of color. It's important to interlock the yarns every time they meet as follows:

On a knit row: Drop the old yarn *to the left* of the new one, then pick up the new one *from underneath* the old one, bring it over the new one, and begin knitting (illustration 4).

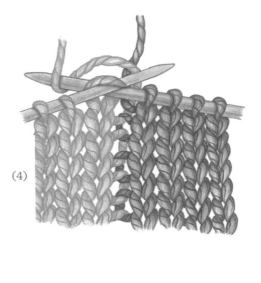

(4)

(2)   (3)

On a purl row: Drop the old yarn *to the left* of the new one, then pick up the new one *from underneath* the old one, bring it over the new one, and begin purling (illustration 5).

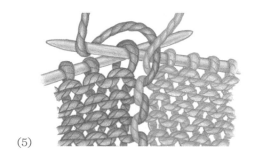

(5)

Knit into the Front and Back of a Stitch (abbreviated K1f&b)

Here's a simple way to increase: First, insert the right-hand needle into the indicated stitch knitwise, wrap the working yarn around the needle the regular way to knit up a stitch *but don't remove the original stitch off the left-hand needle* (illustration 6).

Then, reinsert your right-hand needle, from right to left and *from front to back,* into the back of the same stitch, wrap the yarn around the needle to knit up a stitch (illustration 7), then slip the original stitch off. Two stitches are made out of one stitch.

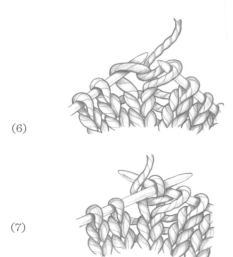

(6)

(7)

K2tog Decrease

Here's the simplest kind of decrease, and the resulting stitch slants toward the right. To do it, simply insert your right-hand knitting needle into 2 stitches at once instead of 1 stitch, and knit them together as 1 stitch (illustration 8).

Note: For a k3tog, use this same method to combine 3 stitches into 1 stitch.

(8)

Knit a Stitch Through Its Back Loop (abbreviated k1-tbl)

This technique twists a stitch. It is often used to create texture in fabric as in the ribbed strap on Sausalito on page 83. To work this technique, just insert your right-hand needle into the indicated stitch from right to left and *from front to back,* and wrap the working yarn around the needle the regular way to knit the stitch.

Knitwise

Instructions will sometimes tell you to insert your knitting needle into a stitch knitwise. To do this, simply insert the tip of your right-hand needle into the indicated stitch as if you were about to knit that stitch—in other words, from left to right and *from front to back* (illustration 9).

(9)

If you're told to slip a stitch knitwise, insert the tip of your right-hand needle into the indicated stitch as if you're about to knit it and slide that stitch off of the left-hand needle and onto the right-hand one, allowing the stitch to sit on the right-hand needle with its left "leg" in the front. Usually, stitches are slipped knitwise during a decrease.

Magic Ball

See page 21.

Make One Increase (abbreviated M1)

This method of increasing is the most invisible and therefore perhaps the most useful one to have in your knitting backpack. It can be made knitwise or purlwise, depending on how the stitch will eventually be worked on the subsequent row. If not specified, the knitwise version is assumed.

To M1 knitwise, use the left-hand needle to scoop up the horizontal strand that's hanging between the needles *from front to back*, and knit the strand *through its back loop*, twisting it to prevent a hole in your fabric (illustration 10).

(10)

To M1 purlwise, use the left-hand needle to scoop up the horizontal strand that's hanging between the needles *from front to back*, and purl the strand *through its back loop*, twisting it to prevent a hole in your fabric.

P2tog Decrease

This technique combines 2 purl stitches into 1 stitch, and it's usually worked on wrong-side rows; the resulting stitch slants toward the right on the right side of the fabric.

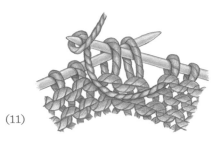

(11)

To do this decrease, simply insert your right-hand knitting needle into 2 stitches at once and purl them together as 1 stitch (illustration 11).

Note: For a p3tog, use the same method to combine 3 stitches into 1 stitch.

Provisional Cast-on

Using smooth waste yarn in a contrasting color to your working yarn, crochet a loose chain that is 4 or 5 chains longer than the number of stitches you plan to cast on.

Cut the yarn and pull the end through the last chain made to secure it. Tie a loose knot on this tail to mark it as the one you'll use to later unravel the chain.

Turn the crocheted chain over and use a knitting needle to pick up and knit 1 stitch through the back loop of each crocheted chain (illustration 12) until you have cast on the appropriate number of stitches for your knitted piece.

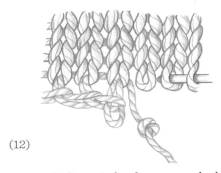

(12)

To expose the live stitches later on, undo the last chain (the one nearest the knotted tail), and gently unzip the entire chain (illustration 13). Transfer the live stitches onto a knitting needle and continue working. Since you'll be knitting on the opposite side of the crocheted chain, you may need to add a stitch at one edge of the knitting to get the correct stitch count.

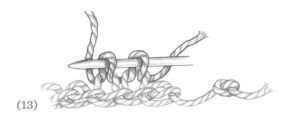

(13)

Purl a Stitch Through Its Back Loop (abbreviated p1-tbl)

Like knitting a stitch through the back loop, this technique twists a stitch. It is often used to create texture in fabric as in the ribbed strap on Sausalito on page 83. To work this technique, just insert your right-hand needle into the indicated stitch from left to right and *from back to front,* and wrap the working yarn around the needle the regular way to purl the stitch.

Purlwise

When instructed to insert your knitting needle into a stitch purlwise, simply insert the tip of your right-hand needle into the indicated stitch as if you were about to purl that stitch—in other words, from right to left and *from back to front* (illustration 14).

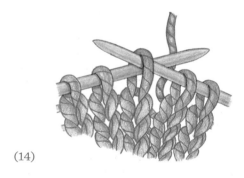

(14)

The convention in knitting is to always slip stitches purlwise unless told otherwise. When told to slip a stitch purlwise, insert the tip of your right-hand needle into the indicated stitch as if you're about to purl it and slide that stitch off of the left-hand needle and onto the right-hand one, allowing the stitch to sit on the right-hand needle with its right "leg" in the front.

Russian Join

See page 22.

Ssk Decrease

This decrease—known as "slip, slip, knit"—slants toward the left. It requires two steps to complete.

First slip 2 stitches *knitwise, one at a time,* from the left-hand needle onto the right-hand one (illustration 15).

Then insert the tip of the left-hand needle into the fronts of these 2 stitches and knit them together from this position (illustration 16).

Note: For an sssk decrease, use the same method, but slip 3 stitches rather than 2 stitches, and then knit them together into 1 stitch.

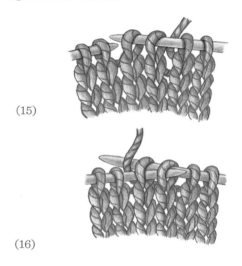

(15)

(16)

Ssp Decrease

Here's a decrease that's most often used on wrong-side rows; the resulting stitch slants toward the left on the right side.

Slip 2 stitches *knitwise, one at a time,* from the left-hand needle onto the right-hand one. Then slip them back to the left-hand needle, keeping them twisted.

Then insert the tip of the right-hand needle *through the back loops* of the 2 stitches (going into the second stitch first) and purl them together from this position (illustration 17).

(17)

Note: For an sssp decrease, use the same method, but slip 3 stitches rather than 2 stitches, and then purl them together into 1 stitch.

Stranded Technique

In this color knitting technique, 2 colors are worked across each row, and when a color is not in use, it is carried loosely across the wrong side of the fabric, creating horizontal floats. Knitters can choose among three possible methods for holding the yarn:

Holding One Color in Each Hand: Here's the most efficient way to work stranded knitting: Hold one yarn in each hand, wrapping them around your fingers to control the tension the way you normally do (illustration 18). To work a stitch with the color from the right-hand yarn, insert the needle into the next stitch knitwise or purlwise according to your pattern, wrap the right-hand yarn around the needle to make either a knit or purl stitch; to make a stitch with the color of the yarn you're holding in your left hand, insert the needle into the next stitch knitwise or purlwise depending on your pattern, and wrap the left-hand yarn around the needle to complete the stitch.

(18)

Holding Both Colors in the Right Hand: If you're normally an American-style "thrower," you can put both yarns in your right hand and use the appropriate color to knit or purl each stitch. Knitters have two possible methods to choose from.

Method 1: Loop both yarns around the right index finger (illustration 19). Use the bend of the top joint of your finger to keep the two yarns apart.

(19)

Method 2: Hold one color yarn over the index finger and the other color yarn over the middle finger (illustration 20).

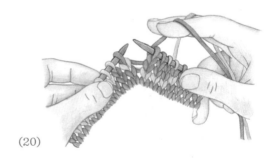

(20)

Holding Both Colors in the Left Hand: If you typically knit Continental-style, you can work with both yarns in your left hand. Again, knitters have two possible methods to choose from. With either method, the right-hand needle can easily "pick" the yarn called for in the color pattern.

Method 1: Place both color yarns over the left index finger (illustration 21). Use the bend of the top joint of your finger to keep the two yarns apart.

(21)

Method 2: Put one color yarn over the left index finger and the other color yarn over the middle finger (illustration 22).

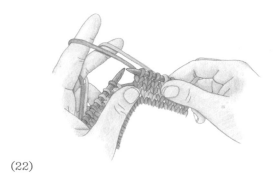

(22)

Three-Needle Bind-off

Some knitters use this technique to bind off and join their shoulder seams at the same time. If your sweater is particularly heavy, I don't recommend it. The resulting seam is quite stretchy and your garment will surely grow—uncontrollably—in length. In this book, I use this type of seam to finish off the top of the hood on page 119. It's practically invisible!

To knit this seam, hold the pieces with their right sides together. With one set of stitches on one needle and the other stitches on a second needle, insert a third knitting needle knitwise into the first stitch on each of the other

two needles, wrap the working yarn around them, and knit the stitches together as if they're one stitch.

Slip the new stitch off onto the right-hand needle.

Insert the third needle knitwise into the next 2 stitches on the left-hand needles, and knit the stitches together, slipping the new stitch off onto the right-hand needle (illustration 23).

Pass the first stitch on the right-hand needle over the second stitch to bind it off.

Continue across the row, knitting together one stitch from each left-hand needle and binding off as you go.

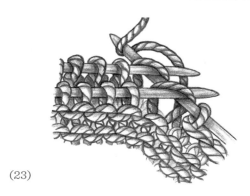

(23)

Yarn Over Increase

This type of increase creates a decorative hole in knitted fabric and is most often used to make lace and other openwork patterns. It is done differently depending on whether the next stitch to be worked will be knitted or purled.

For a yarn over *immediately before a knit stitch,* bring the working yarn to the front, between the tips of the knitting needles. As you knit the next stitch, the yarn will go over the right-hand needle to create the extra stitch.

For a yarn over *immediately before a purl stitch,* the working yarn must be brought to the front, between the tips of the knitting needles, and then wrapped *completely around* the right-hand needle and back to the front.

FINISHING TECHNIQUES

Basic Fringe

Fringe can stabilize the edge of a piece of knitting and is a simple decorative addition to any project!

First, cut a piece of cardboard to your desired fringe length. Wind the yarn *loosely* around the cardboard the number of times specified in the pattern, and then cut across one end.

Hold several strands together and fold in half. With the right side of your project facing you, use a crochet hook to draw the folded end from the right side to the wrong side on the edge of your project (illustration 24).

Pull the loose ends through the folded loop, then tighten the knot.

Trim the fringe evenly after all tufts are attached.

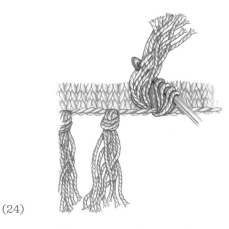

(24)

Note: To attach additional strands of fringe to hide an existing yarn tail (as in Tamara's Wrap on page 97), just grab the existing tail and pull it through the folded loop.

Blocking

Prior to seaming your knitted pieces, take the time to block them into shape. You'll be surprised at how this simple process can improve the appearance of your projects and can tame even the most unruly stitches! To do it, follow the laundering instructions on the yarn label for the most delicate yarn in your project, then use rustless pins to shape the damp fabric to your desired measurements and allow it to dry. Or gently steam the pieces into shape by placing a damp cloth over them and then carefully wafting a hot steam iron just above the fabric. Don't actually touch the iron to the fabric or you'll risk flattening it.

Hiding Yarn Tails

Use a pointed-end yarn needle to make short running stitches on the wrong side of your fabric in a diagonal line for about 1"/[2.5cm] or so, piercing the yarn strands that comprise the stitches of your fabric. Then work back again to where you began, stitching alongside your previous running stitches. Finally, to secure the tail, work a stitch or two and actually pierce the running stitches you just created. Be sure to work each tail individually, in opposite diagonal directions, and you will secure your yarn ends while keeping the public side of your fabric neat and beautiful.

Mattress Stitch Seams

Here's the neatest seam imaginable for stockinette stitch and most knitted fabrics. Nearly invisible, it can be worked vertically or horizontally.

For a Vertical Seam: Lay your pieces flat, with the right sides of the fabric facing you, matching patterns and stripes, if applicable.

Thread a blunt-end yarn needle with your sewing yarn, then bring the needle up *from back to front* through the left-hand piece of fabric, going in one stitch from the edge, leaving a 6"/[15cm] tail.

Bring the yarn up and through the corresponding spot on the right-hand piece to secure the lower edges.

Insert the needle *from front to back* into the same spot on the left-hand piece where the needle emerged last time and bring it up through the corresponding place of the next row of knitting.

Insert the needle *from front to back* into the same spot on the right-hand piece where the needle emerged last time and bring it up through the corresponding place of the next row of knitting.

Repeat the last two steps until you've sewn approximately 2"/[5cm], then pull firmly on the sewing yarn to bring the pieces of the fabric together, allowing the 2 stitches on the edges of each piece to roll to the wrong side. Continue this way until your seam is complete (illustration 25).

(25)

For a Horizontal Seam: Lay your pieces flat with the right sides of the fabric facing you and with the bound-off edges of the pieces together. Bring the needle up through the center of a stitch just below the bound-off edge on the lower piece of fabric, then insert it *from front to back* and *from right to left* around both legs of the corresponding stitch on the other piece of fabric. Bring the needle tip back down through the center of the same stitch where it first emerged. Continue this way until your seam is complete (illustration 26).

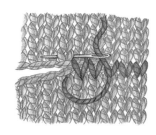

(26)

Sewing In a Zipper

Don't be afraid to add a zipper to a sweater! It's easy to do—and fun and convenient to wear. With the zipper closed and the right side of the garment pieces facing you, pin the zipper into place, keeping in mind that

with hairier fabrics it might be best to allow more of the teeth to show, so the fibers don't get caught in the zipper's operation. Use contrasting sewing thread to baste the zipper into place (illustration 27).

Remove the pins, and with matching sewing thread, whipstitch the tape to the wrong side (illustration 28). Finally, with the right side of the garment facing you, use back stitch to sew down the zipper tape neatly (illustration 29). Fold any excess zipper tape to the wrong side and tack it down.

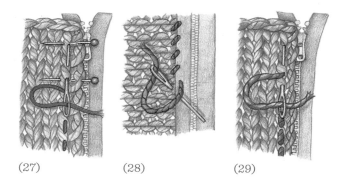

(27)   (28)   (29)

Sweater Assembly

Sweater pieces fit together like a jigsaw puzzle, with the type of armhole determining how the front, back, and sleeves interlock. Refer to the illustrations below when assembling sweaters.

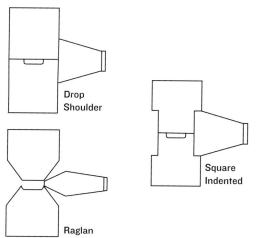

Drop Shoulder

Raglan

Square Indented

knitting charts

At first glance, knitting charts might seem to be an exotic secret code drawn mysteriously on a grid. Actually, they are terrific tools that can make reading and knitting patterns faster and easier than long paragraphs of text. Like foreign languages, knitting charts and their symbols are simple to translate once you become familiar with the "grammar" and "vocabulary."

A QUICK LESSON IN GRAMMAR

Designers and publications use knitting charts as visual representations of finished knitted fabric.

Each square of the grid corresponds to one stitch, and each row of squares corresponds to one row of stitches.

Charts are read in the same way that the fabric is usually knit—from the lower edge up, with the first row at the bottom of the chart and the last row at the top.

Right-side rows are read from right to left, in the same order that stitches present themselves to you on the left-hand knitting needle. Illustration 1 shows the order that stitches will be worked for Row 1, a right-side row, in a chart.

Of course, at the end of this first row, you turn your knitting before starting the next row, and the wrong side of the fabric faces you. Physically, the first stitch of this wrong-side row is the same stitch as the very last stitch of the right-side row you just finished. For this reason, wrong-side rows on charts are read in the opposite direction, from left to right, from left to right (illustration 2).

Charts make it easy to see how many stitches are involved in a pattern. In some charts, bold vertical lines indicate the stitch repeat, and if extra stitches are required on each side to center the pattern on the fabric, they are shown to the left and right of the repeat. In the Keiki Baby Kimono on page 45, for example, both zigzag patterns have a multiple of 6 plus 1 stitches; the chart shows a six-stitch repeat with a "balancing" stitch on one side

To read the chart below, for example, you'd start at the lower right-hand corner, read from right to left, work the four stitches between the two bold lines as many times as is necessary to get across your fabric, and end the row with the stitch represented in this sample chart by the star. This stitch sits outside the stitch repeat and so is worked once per row. It is the last stitch of every right-side row, and since wrong-side rows are read from left to right, it is the first stitch of these rows.

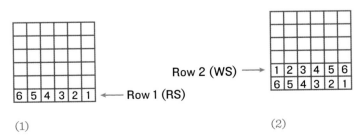

(1)

Row 2 (WS) →

Row 1 (RS)

(2)

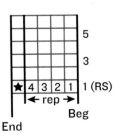

End

THE VOCABULARY LIST

Each symbol on a chart describes how a stitch or group of stitches will be worked, and the arrangement of symbols on the chart determines the stitch pattern.

Usually, the symbols visually resemble the way the resulting stitches will appear on the public side of the knitted fabric. This means there's no need for memorization by you! It's relatively intuitive to use the symbols. The symbol for a knit stitch, for example, is a blank box, mimicking the flat appearance of the knit stitch itself; the dot symbol for a purl stitch depicts the bumpy appearance of a purled stitch.

A symbol that occupies several squares of the grid indicates the number of stitches that will be involved in that particular knitting maneuver. Cables, obviously, are worked over more than one stitch, so cable symbols occupy several adjacent squares. In the charts in this book, each line or dot within every cable symbol represents one of the stitches being crossed, so you can quickly tell at a glance the number of stitches involved. For instance, three lines crossing three other lines would symbolize a six-stitch cable. In the cabled Boho Bangle on page 31, for instance, three lines crossing three other lines symbolize a six-stitch cable. Easy!

Designers and editors may use different sets of symbols to represent the same knitting maneuvers, but they are usually variations on a theme. Just think about them as unique "dialects" of this "foreign language"! In this book, all symbols resemble the resulting stitch, so reading them is quite intuitive. And don't forget that there's always a stitch key nearby, so the symbols are easy to decipher.

All rows in charts are shown as they appear on the public side of the fabric. Consequently, the same symbol means different things on right-side and wrong-side rows. The blank box, for instance, represents a knit stitch on a right-side row, but if you're on a wrong-side row and want the stitch to appear as a knit stitch on the reverse side of the fabric, you must purl it.

If a symbol is used on both right- and wrong-side rows of the chart, the stitch key will tell you which knitting maneuver to use where.

Usually, wrong-side rows are pretty simple: You just knit the knit stitches and purl the purl stitches as they present themselves to you on the knitting needle. Scan the entire chart before you begin knitting to confirm that this is the case. If so, you can zip along those wrong-side rows reading your knitting rather than the chart!

It might take some practice—and a little patience—to begin to knit from charts. But once you get the hang of it, I bet you'll prefer them over long, wordy instructions. Trust me!

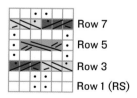

Row 7

Row 5

Row 3

Row 1 (RS)

Key   ☐ = K on RS; p on WS

• = P on RS; k on WS

= Slip 2 sts onto cn and hold in front; p1; k2 from cn

= Slip 1 st onto cn and hold in back; k2; p1 from cn

= Slip 2 sts onto cn and hold in front; k2; k2 from cn

tips

- Enlarge your charts on a copy machine to make reading them easier.

- If you're an exceptionally visual person, use a color key to simplify reading the symbols: Choose a different color highlighting pen for each symbol in your key and throughout the chart (as in the example). Instead of deciphering each symbol individually, you'll have your own useful color code!

- Place stitch markers on your knitting needles to separate each pattern repeat or panel.

- Use a row counter to keep track of where you are on the chart.

glossary of symbols

Every chart in this book has a symbol key nearby, but for handy reference, here's a list of every symbol used in charts in this book.

☐ = K on RS; p on WS

• = P on RS; k on WS

o = Yarn over

⟋ = K2tog

⟍ = Ssk

⟩⟨ = Right Twist = Slip next st onto cn and hold in back; k1; k1 from cn **or** k2tog, leaving them on LH needle; insert point of RH needle between these 2 sts and k the first st again

⟩⟩⟨ = Slip 2 stitches onto cn and hold in back; k1; k2 from cn

⟩⟨⟨ = Slip next st onto cn and hold in front; k2; k1 from cn

⟩⟩⟨⟨ = Slip 2 sts onto cn and hold in back; k2; k2 from cn

⟩⟩⟨⟨ = Slip 2 sts onto cn and hold in front; k2; k2 from cn

⟩⟩⟩⟨⟨⟨ = Slip 3 sts onto cn and hold in back; k3; k3 from cn

⟩⟩⟩⟨⟨⟨ = Slip 3 sts onto cn and hold in front; k3; k3 from cn

V = K1f&b=Knit into the front and back of next stitch

M = M1 knitwise

⊗ = Bobble = Knit into (front, back, front) of next st, turn; p1, (p1, yarn over, p1) all into next st, p1, turn; k5, turn; p2tog, p1, p2tog, turn; slip 2 sts at once knitwise, k1, p2sso

abbreviations

Following is a list of abbreviations used in the charts of this book. Many of the techniques are discussed in the Knitting Techniques section (page 128).

beg   beg(inning)

cm   centimeter(s)

cn   cable needle

g   gram(s)

k   knit

k1f&b   knit into the front and back of a stitch (increase)

k1-tbl   knit next stitch through its back loop

k2tog   knit the next 2 stitches together; this is a right-slanting decrease

LH   left-hand

m   meter(s)

mm   millimeter(s)

M1   make 1 (increase)

oz   ounce(s)

p   purl

p1-tbl   purl next stitch through its back loop

p2tog   purl the next 2 stitches together; this is a right-slanting decrease

RH   right-hand

rnd(s)   round(s)

rpt   repeat

RS   right side (of work)

ssk   slip the next 2 stitches knitwise, one at a time from the left-hand needle to the right-hand one, insert the left-hand needle tip into the fronts of both slipped stitches to knit them together from this position; this is a left-slanting decrease

ssp   slip the next 2 stitches knitwise, one at a time from the left-hand needle to the right-hand one, return both stitches to left-hand needle and insert the right-hand needle into them from left to right and from back to front, to purl them together through their back loops; this is a left-slanting decrease

st(s)   stitch(es)

WS   wrong side (of work)

yd(s)   yard(s)

yo   yarn over

*   repeat instructions after asterisk or between the asterisks across the row or for as many times as instructed

( )   alternate measurements and/or instructions for different sizes; also, repeat the instructions within parentheses for as many times as instructed

[ ]   repeat the instructions within bracket for as many times as instructed; these brackets also indicate the separation between empirical and metric measurements in the pattern text

resources

I always recommend purchasing supplies at your local yarn shop. If there isn't one in your area, contact the appropriate wholesaler listed here for more information.

Adriafil
See Plymouth Yarns.

The Alpaca Yarn Company
144 Roosevelt Ave.
York, PA 17401
(717) 848-5842
www.thealpacayarnco.com

Aurora Yarns
PO Box 3068
Moss Beach, CA 94038
(650) 728-2730
www.aurorayarns.net

Blue Sky Alpacas
PO Box 88
Cedar, MN 55011
(763) 753-5815
www.blueskyalpacas.com

Brown Sheep Company
100662 County Road 16
Mitchell, NE 69357
(308) 635-2198
www.brownsheep.com

Cascade Yarns
1224 Andover Park E
Tukwila, WA 98188
(206) 574-0440
www.cascadeyarns.com

Classic Elite Yarns
122 Western Avenue
Lowell, MA 01851
(978) 453-2837
www.classiceliteyarns.com

JCA, Inc.
35 Scales Lane
Townsend, MA 01469
(978) 597-8794
www.jcacrafts.com

Jamieson's Wools
See Simply Shetland.

Louet North America
3425 Hands Road
Prescott, Ontario CANADA
K0E 1T0
(613) 925-4502
www.louet.com

Malabrigo Yarn
Gaboto 1277
Montevideo, 11200 URUGUAY
(786) 866-6187
www.malabrigoyarn.com

Mission Falls
5333 Casgrain, 1204
Montreal, Quebec CANADA
H2T 1X3
(877) 244-1204
www.missionfalls.com

One World Button Supply Company
41 Union Square West, Suite 311
New York, NY 10003
(212) 691-1331
www.oneworldbuttons.com

Ornaghi Filati Yarns
See Aurora Yarns.

Plymouth Yarn Company
500 Lafayette Street
PO Box 28
Bristol, PA 19007
(215) 788-0459
www.plymouthyarn.com

Reynolds Yarn
See JCA, Inc.

Rowan Yarn
See Westminster Fibers.

Simply Shetland
18375 Olympic Avenue South
Seattle, WA 98188
(877) 743-8526
http://simplyshetland.net

Westminster Fibers
165 Ledge St.
Nashua, NH 03060
(603) 886-5041
www.westminsterfibers.com

THE KNITTING COMMUNITY

The Knitting Guild Association
I currently sit on their advisory board and can attest to the educational value—and pure knitterly fun—of this group. To meet other knitters and learn more, contact
1100-H Brandywine Boulevard
Zanesville, OH 43701-7303
(740) 452-4541
e-mail: TKGA@TKGA.com
www.tkga.com

www.ravelry.com
Another popular venue to meet other knitters online.

acknowledgments

Special thanks go to the following knitters for helping to make the samples for this book:

Marie Duquette, Lynn Gates, Toni Gill, Cindy Grosch, Nancy Hand, Tom Jensen, Cheryl Keeley, Amy Maceyko, Robin May, Joan Murphy, Judy Seip, Melony Sorbero, Norma Jean Sternschein, and Angie Tzoumakas. I couldn't have done this project without you.

I greatly value the opportunity to work once again with two brilliant stars in the knitting industry: Charlotte Quiggle and Joni Coniglio. Your work behind the scenes—and at all hours of the day and night—makes so many authors and designers look good. Thank you!

Many thanks to my dear friend Jocelyn Grayson, who read through parts of this manuscript in its earliest form. It is a better book because of your input!

Thanks, too, to all the yarn companies I've worked with throughout the years. Your generosity has made my work (and my stash) amazingly colorful and full of inspiration!

Much affection and gratitude to Ken Wing for his patience and love (not to mention all the Indian buffet lunches!) while I worked on this project. Aloha no au ia ʻoe.

index

Note: Page numbers in *italics* indicate patterns.